ON THE LINE

Published by Black Inc.,
an imprint of Schwartz Books Pty Ltd
Level 1, 221 Drummond Street
Carlton VIC 3053, Australia
enquiries@blackincbooks.com
www.blackincbooks.com

Originally published in France in 2019 as *À la ligne: Feuillets d'usine*
English translation by Stephanie Smee, 2021
This edition published in 2021

9781760642334 (paperback)
9781743821435 (ebook)

NATIONAL LIBRARY OF AUSTRALIA
A catalogue record for this book is available from the National Library of Australia

Cover design by Akiko Chan
Text design and typesetting by Akiko Chan

Printed in Australia by McPherson's Printing Group.

MIX
Paper from responsible sources
FSC® C001695
FSC www.fsc.org

Australian Government
Australia Council for the Arts

This project has been assisted by the Australian Government through the Australia Council, its arts funding and advisory body.

JOSEPH PONTHUS

ON THE LINE

NOTES FROM A FACTORY

Translated by Stephanie Smee

Black Inc.

TRANSLATOR'S NOTE

It is a rare thing indeed to be entrusted with the translation of such a startlingly original work as Joseph Ponthus' *À la ligne*.

It is a work that bears reading and rereading. A work that I hope will sit with you, its new Anglophone audience, as it has sat with me while working with Ponthus' words, laughing at his black humour, reeling at some of his descriptions and wondering at the gentle but persistent thread of humanity that winds its way through the text.

A brief comment on the title. A clever double entendre in the French, *à la ligne* can mean 'on the line' in the context of a production line, but any reader who has ever done French dictation will also recognise the instruction to start a new line of text, or perhaps to press 'return' on a keyboard.

With each new phrase, the author 'returns' to a new line, as he returns to the factory, producing a rhythm that matches the relentlessness of the production line. Yet it is a technique that also allows the creation of a visual space on the page which, in turn, might be seen as reflecting that place in one's mind, that mental and spiritual retreat which allows us to preserve our humanity and continue to engage when confronted with the most challenging of circumstances.

Readers might also be interested in the endnotes included in this edition after Ponthus' text. They are in no way meant to represent a complete glossary; rather they elucidate some of the more specific cultural assumptions and political references with which Anglophones may not be as familiar as their French counterparts.

I add my thanks here to the team at Black Inc., and in particular to Sophy Williams and Jo Rosenberg for sharing my enthusiasm for this work and for their support. And to my early readers, Sophie Masson, Michael Smee, Kate Morgan, Paul Schoff and Julia Gentil, for their comments.

Most importantly, thank you to you, Joseph, and to Alice Déon at La Table Ronde for the opportunity to work on this special text. I can only hope that its new readers are as captivated and moved as I have been when preparing this translation. Perhaps then I will know if I have done it justice.

Stephanie Smee

This book

Which is for Krystel and which owes everything to her

Is dedicated in a spirit of solidarity

To the working classes in every country
To the uneducated and to the 'sans-dents'
The so-called toothless of our society
Alongside whom I have
Learned laughed suffered and worked
So much

To Charles Trenet
Without whose songs
I would not have held out

To M.D.G.

and

To my mother

PART ONE

‘It is fantastic what one can endure.’

Guillaume Apollinaire

(letter to Madeleine Pagès, 30 November 1915)

1.

Entering the factory
Of course I was ready for
The stench
The cold
The shifting of heavy loads
The harshness of it all
The conditions
The production line
The modern slavery

I wasn't there to report on it
Nor was I readying myself for the revolution
No
The factory means I get to earn a buck
Put food on the table
As the saying goes
Because my wife is sick of seeing me lounge around
on the couch waiting for a job in my field
So it's
The agro-industrial plant for me
Food processing
The agro industry
As they say
A factory in Brittany
Handling processing cooking and all things fish
and prawns
I'm not there to write
I'm there for the money

At the temp agency they ask me when I can start
I pull out the Victor Hugo
My usual literary go-to
Tried and tested
'Tomorrow at dawn when the countryside pales I guess'
They take me at my word and the next day I clock on at
six in the morning

As the hours and days go by the need to write embeds
itself like a bone in my throat I can't dislodge
But not of the grimness of the factory
Rather its paradoxical beauty

On my production line I often find myself thinking of a
parable
One of Claudel's I'm pretty sure
A man makes a pilgrimage from Paris to Chartres and
comes across a fellow busy breaking stones
What are you doing
My job
Breaking these shitty rocks
My back's done in
It's a dog's job
Shouldn't be allowed
Would sooner die
Some kilometres further on a second fellow's busy
doing the same job
Same question
I'm working
I've got a family to feed
It's a bit tough

That's just how it is and at least I've got a job
That's the main thing
Further on still
Outside Chartres
A third man
His face radiant
What are you doing
I'm building a cathedral

May the prawns and fish be my stones

At first the smell of the factory irritated my nostrils
Now I no longer notice it
The cold is bearable with a big jumper a hoodie two
decent pairs of socks and leggings under my pants
Shifting the heavy loads
I'm finding muscles I didn't know existed
I am willing in my servitude
Happy almost

The factory has taken me
I refer to it now only as
My factory
As if I had some form of ownership of the machines
or proprietary interest in the processing of the prawns
and fish
Small-time casual worker that I am
One among so many others
Soon
We'll be processing shellfish too
Crabs lobsters spider crabs and crayfish

That's a revolution I'm hoping to see
Hoping to bag some claws even if I already know it
won't be possible
It's bad enough trying to filch just a single prawn
You've really got to hide if you want to eat a few
I'm still too obvious my co-worker Brigitte
an older woman has said to me
'I didn't see anything but watch it if the bosses catch
you'
So now I sneak them out under my apron with my hands
triple gloved to keep out the moisture the cold and
everything else so I can peel and eat what I consider at
the very least to be some form of payment in kind

I'm getting ahead of myself
Back to the writing
'I write as I speak when the fiery angel of conversation
takes hold of me like a prophet' wrote Barbey
d'Aurevilly or something along those lines somewhere
I'm not quite sure where
I write like I think when I'm on my production line
Mind wandering alone determined
I write like I work
On the production line
Return
New line

Clocking on
It's just an endless white corridor
Cold

With punch clocks at one end where people flock at night when it's time to clock on
Four o'clock
Six o'clock
Half past seven in the morning
Depending on the job you've been given
Unloading which means emptying crates of fish
Sorting or scaling and skinning which means cutting the fish up
Cooking which means anything to do with the prawns

I haven't yet had the misfortune of doing an afternoon or evening shift
Of starting at four and finishing at midnight
Here
Everybody says
And so far I agree
That the earlier you start
The better it is – not counting the night hours with their twenty percent loading
That way 'you get your afternoon'
'If you're going to get up early anyway
Might as well get up really early'
My arse
Your eight hours of slog
Means eight hours of slog whatever the time of day
And then
When you leave
At knock-off time
You go home
You bum around

You pass out
You're already thinking about the time you need to set the alarm
Doesn't really matter what time
It'll always be too early
After the sleep of the dead
It's morning smokes and coffee downed
At the factory
And you're slammed straight back into it
As if there's no transition from the night-time world
You re-enter in a dream
Or a nightmare
In the neon light
You're on autopilot
Thoughts drifting
In waking half-sleep
Pulling heaving sorting carrying lifting weighing cleaning
Like when you're falling asleep
Not even trying to work out why all these actions
All these thoughts are blurred into one
On the line
And the daylight at break time when you get to go out for a smoke and a coffee
It surprises you every time

I know only a few places that have this sort of effect on me
Uncompromising existential radical
Greek sanctuaries
Prisons
Islands

And the factory
When you leave them
You never know if you are returning to the real world
or leaving it behind
Even if we know there's no real world
But it doesn't really matter
Delphi was chosen by Apollo to be the centre of the
world and that wasn't by chance
The Agora was chosen by Athens for the birth of an idea
of the world and that was a necessity
The prison chosen by Foucault was chosen by the prison
itself
Islands were chosen by the light the rain and the wind
The factory was chosen by Marx and the proletariat
Closed worlds
Places you go only by choice
Deliberately
Places you don't leave
How should I say this
You don't leave a sanctuary untouched
You don't ever really leave the slammer
You don't leave an island without a sigh
You don't leave the factory without looking up to the sky

Knock-off time
Such pretty words
Their origin perhaps long forgotten
But understand
In your body
Viscerally
What it really means to knock off

That need to relax to clean yourself off to shower to
wash away the fish scales and recognise the effort it
takes to get up to shower when you've finally sat down
in the garden after eight hours on the line

Tomorrow
It's never a sure thing
Work
As a casual
Contracts run from two days to a week
Tops
It's not Zola but it might as well be
How good it would be to write like it's the 19th century
The age of the heroic worker
But it's the 21st century
I hope for work
I wait to knock off
I wait for work
I hope

Wait and hope
The final words of *Monte Cristo* I realise
My good mate Alexandre Dumas
'Friend, has not the Count just told us the sum of all
human wisdom is contained in these two words: Wait
and hope!'

2.

For whom are we processing forty tonnes a day of
prawns with a use-by date of one month to the day
Every day sixty million French people must eat
forty tonnes of prawns
The factory couldn't operate at a loss if it tried

Four years ago the factory burned down
And was rebuilt in three hundred and sixty-four days
within the prescribed insurance period
People say one of the bosses set fire to it deliberately
Twice
How do you burn down a factory where the maximum
temperature is eight degrees Celsius
You'd have to want to
You'd really want to have it in for the place

What do my fellow line workers think about as they sort
their prawns what insistent songs clutter their minds or
do they enjoy humming
Sometimes through my earplugs and over the factory's
deafening noise I can pick out the tunes of those
popular singers Balavoine and Véronique Sanson
or Christophe Maé asking where happiness is

Our massive production lines
Machine after machine
Where the prawns are
Defrosted

Sorted
Cooked
Refrigerated
Re-sorted
Packaged
Labelled
Re-re-sorted
Gaping metal bellies
Each with its own name
Coaxial
Ishida
Multivac
Arbor
Bizerba
Each with its specific function

Where are they made
These enormous machines
By whom
Are they made by other machines
In which case where are the factories that make
the machines for our factory
And where then would the factories be with the
machines making the machines used to make the
machines for our factory
It's not the people working the machines
I'm talking about but the paradigm of a machine making
another machine

People say two-thirds of the workers at the factory are
casuals for one-third permanent

You have to ask yourself why given the respective wages
But that's a question for the bosses
Only they would know

Why doesn't that boss with the salt and pepper hair
ever greet anybody when there are others more human
in this mechanised world
What part of the factory machine have we unknowingly
become

The prawns all arrive frozen from
Peru from the Mozambique Channel from India from
Nigeria from Guatemala from Ecuador
Exotic tropical destinations
Flags of convenience maybe
Port trading posts definitely

They all arrive whole except for the 'crown of prawns'
appetisers
A sort of cluster of shelled prawns displayed on a round
plastic platter weighing one hundred and twenty-five
grams to be sold in supermarkets for around five euros
Often we process more than ten thousand prawn crown
appetisers a day with a good twenty or so mini prawns
per crown

Who before us has done all that shelling
Who are the line operators in what countries
What workers
For what wage
What children

Line operators
Faces hidden under protective equipment
Under their masks
What of the lives hidden behind the automaton gestures
Behind the help offered by one worker to another
Behind the mechanical sympathy of those slaving away uncomplaining
The silence shrouding our lives feels right
It's the factory that matters
The factory and our monthly wage

So many prawns
So many questions

Tomorrow
'Oh! Vessels of the Danaïdes'
To quote Apollinaire
Bottomless wells of forty-odd tonnes of prawns
Everyday
I'll go back to my factory
Return to the prawns
I'll be at your side
At the brusque treatment of those who have only their labour to sell
Their wind to break
Their filthy jokes at six in the morning
Oh workers of the factory
Whatever they're singing
Whatever existential questions they might be asking themselves
Or not

As they sort their prawns
Whatever questions about life the universe and
everything about nothing about literature about
everything else about prawns
It ultimately comes down to the same thing
Eight hours a day and night on the machines

The word prawn was first used in its current form by
Rabelais
That much I know
It makes me smile and goes with the lingering gastric
stench of the factory

Leave the factory and emerge into the warmth of the
sun if there is any
Have a smoke
Head home
Drink
Fuck
Weep
Laugh
Live a life other than one dictated by a prawn
Sleep
Set the alarm
Sleep the sleep of the dead

Tomorrow it's back to the prawns

3.

On Monday I clock on at four in the morning.

Not on prawns but at the fish market
Four in the morning when the fishermen from the island
of Houat from Le Guilvinec from Douarnenez or some
other place head out to sea
I feel a flash of pride
The market catch is almost certainly a big haul of
sardines
Last time there was a ten-tonne haul to sort then pack in
polystyrene crates full of ice after sticking on the label
'Product of France' attesting to the origin of the catch
It's summer and there'll be much more than the ten
tonnes of the last haul
Have to fill the barbecues
I'll be making sure the mackerel and smelt are removed
Four in the morning get up two hours earlier some
strong coffee prepared last night take the bike for the
requisite half-hour of pedalling
I'll no doubt have Vatel on my mind as I ride
The chef who killed himself over a late delivery of fish
for his boss Louis XIV
If I'm late a little past four in the morning my future will
be no brighter than that of comrade Vatel
Monday
Four in the morning
At the fish market

4.

There's a casual who turned up at the start of the week
and he's worth his weight in sardines

Not content with just being a slack-arse
Bumming ciggies
Scrounging a ride to and from work
Best thing of all he's as sensitive to the cold as he's
allergic to common sense

'It's frickin' freezing in this factory'
'It's a fresh fish plant so yes it's just as well'
'But I'm wearing three pairs of gloves and my hands are
frozen'
'…'
'D'you think I can ask the boss if we can put hot water in
the fish crates where the ice is so it'd be easier to handle'

The good fellow doesn't seem to have worked out what
sauce he'd like on his fish

Nor what work is either for that matter

5.

The unpackers
They're a bit like workers out of the General Workers'
Union handbook
Not part of the mob
A cushier job
With considerable benefits
Compared to the other workers at the factory

You're allowed to arrive five minutes late
When you clock on at four in the morning
The room temperature at eight degrees Celsius feels
almost mild

You get two regulation breaks rather than one imposed
by the boss
Short ten-minute smoke-o and coffee break at six
Half an hour at eight-thirty
More smokes more coffee

The job isn't so tough
Repetitive
Emptying twenty-five-kilo crates of fish so you can fill
more twenty-five-kilo crates
Almost a touch of the Dilberts
But it's a factory
And you build up your muscles

The machinery never breaks down
And the fish change
Pollock whiting black pollock and yellow pollock
scabbard fish haddock monkfish and yet more pollock
of every description
It keeps the repetition and monotony at bay

Today the unpackers were striking
Nobody else at the factory
Proof of privilege of benefits acquired
Benefits that must have been hard-won
Good luck to them

There were just the two of us casuals when it was time
to clock on
Some guys came to lend us a hand after the first break
We unpacked crates and crates of scabbard fish and
whiting
We got the job done

As I write these words
I continue
To offload rather than unload
More bollocks perhaps than
Pollocks

6.

Today in between the several tonnes of scabbard fish
grenadiers and pollock
I unpacked three hundred and fifty kilos of chimera fish
I didn't even know such a fish existed until this morning

My chimera arrived after the break
Funny-looking fish with two handsome fins on its
underbelly resembling wings you might say
Perhaps that's where it gets its name
Or not

That morning it was enough to make me happy
That I could say I had unpacked chimeras

I stop by the temp agency that afternoon
It's the 31st and I want to pick up my advance
Seeing as we're required by regulation to be paid on the
11th of the following month an advance is payable
Up to seventy-five percent of hours worked
Human resources at the factory have not yet signed off
on my hours from my last week of work
So I'm paid fifty percent of what I'm owed

Yet another chimera

7.

At the factory today
I unpack quite a few grenadiers

At the factory today
Quite a few co-workers fancy themselves as grenadiers
In the military sense of the word

After the horror of the Nice attack when a truck
ploughed into the July 14 crowd
Some would like a special dispensation for 'ragheads'
on their hunting licence

Some would like to put them all on a boat in the Atlantic
and boom just like that our fish would have plenty to eat

A lot of them agree with the idea of vigilantism seeing as
the cops they say are useless

Fabrice Le Noxaïc
The one who wants to organise himself a special
'raghead' hunting licence
Systematically marks his initials with a black felt pen
on his equipment boots work coats trousers gloves but
starting with his surname namely LNF

I get a kick out of thinking it would pretty much kill him
To have to write out the letters FLN
And be reminded of the *Front de Libération Nationale*

Perhaps he's sorry not to be called Olivier-Antoine
Schultz
And have the initials of the *Organisation de l'Armée*
Secrète

8.

I've found a job just for a month in the sector
I was originally trained for
And for the first time in my life
I'll be one of the bosses

Except that
Just like we're 'line operators' now and not 'workers'
I won't be a 'boss' but a 'manager'

Overseeing a dozen holiday camps as it happens
Spread over a huge area from Paris to Belgium and
Adapted for 'people living with a disability'
We don't use the word 'handicapped' now and certainly
not 'retard'

Company car hotels expense accounts if everything
pans out

Endlessly on the road if a problem crops up and I'm
six hundred clicks away

But that's not the point of the story

Today I had training in some out of the way hole of
a village in the Brittany boondocks the centre of the
arsehole of the world to get ready for the business of
being a boss and to meet my future teams of holiday
camp supervisors and group leaders

Let's just say that having to go from the rhythm of the factory to that of social workers overnight
Is a bit like going from one particular concept of labour to another concept of labour in the most Marxist sense of the term

Coffee ciggie break coffee ciggie
'Chat with colleagues' ciggie coffee and so on break

Prawns whelks prawns prawns containers more containers yet more bloody prawns wait for the boss to say you can go on break back to the prawns the whelks the prawns the prawns

Both cases involve subordination and the sale of my labour power

My weekday job of lowly labourer
Becomes that of boss this Saturday

One of my future 'colleagues' wants to speak to me privately for a few moments

She's sporting the hippie look fresh from the Vieilles Charrues music fest with hair rolled as tight as her ciggies

'So you're going to be my supervisor'
'Yes'
'No well you see I really believe that the people here for

a holiday should absolutely have a good holiday because
it's their holiday after all'
'...'
'Because I mean how do we feel when we don't get a
good holiday it doesn't really count as a real holiday'

There are some Saturdays you regret not selling your
labour power for prawns and whelks
They at least don't talk back at you

9.

This boss man stuff with the handicapped
It's over

It was a bit like having a three-week WHV
As they say in Quebec
A fourteen-day 'working holiday visa'

I was on the road
A lot

I thought of Louis Aragon's *Conscript from a Hundred Villages*
A melodious rosary of bell-towers and names
From Normandy to Belgium passing Nord-Pas de Calais on the way
I'll never manage to say
Hauts-de-France its new name

I saw plenty of villages and plenty of roads
People not so much

Dunkirk Saint-Valéry-en-Caux Fécamp Berck-sur-Mer
La Roche-Guyon Étampes Trouville
Verviers Westrozebeke and Ostend to see the Belgian cousins Vétheuil Vernon Verneuil-sur-Avre Beuvron-en-Auge

A France of sub-prefectures
Of town squares with cobblestones and half-timbered houses
Of Flemish belfries

The memory of wars

The one from Fourteen
Passchendaele the Somme Péronne the Race to the Sea
Ypres where I missed hearing the Last Post that's played every evening at eight all the English Canadian even Indian and Maori cemeteries seen from a distance 'cos I had to hit the road again

And the one from Thirty-nine in Normandy
Well more Forty-four really

Being on the road
It's almost as repetitive
As sorting the crates the fish the prawns
But different evidently
To the job of supervising people who are slogging away for handicapped holiday makers
I've got nothing much to say about it
Uninteresting
And as for the driving
It's not much better

Some of the things I wanted to see
Flashed by faster than a blitzkrieg
Étretat

Giverny
Honfleur
Postcards drowning in
Flowers from Monet's garden

And the houses of the Erik Satie Museum
One of the most beautiful museums in the world that people had so harped on about
Rightly so
A flying pear
A room in Montmartre
A mechanical piano
A pedal contraption that opens a sort of giant umbrella

Back on the road
On the freeway
Mont-Saint-Michel was catching the glow of the setting sun in the distance
I drove past Villedieu-les-Poêles the village of copper works and its inhabitants said to be deaf from the incessant banging of metal on metal
And said by Rabelais even in his tale of *Gargantua* to have supplied the metal used to make his hero's cutlery
Then it was back to Brittany and home

Where I returned to the dying sound of Breton bagpipes from the Lorient Inter-Celtic Festival
It was the night of the Perseids
Of meteor showers and shooting stars
Faraway fireworks
And I looked to the sky as I made my wish

This morning
I dropped into the temp agency hoping to pick up last month's cheque and a new contract
Bingo
Four weeks of nights in a new factory
From eight-thirty to five-thirty in the morning
I'm done with fish and prawns
But not with the trays the crates and the machines

I sign up again happy despite the stress of the new factory and regretting already my fish and prawns
What will I be processing

I didn't process anything with my handicapped holiday makers
Who themselves are busy processing and making things for the remainder of the year in sheltered workshops
Working for wages as adapted as their holidays but happy and proud
Some tell me of their carpentry and the endless smoothing of furniture with strokes of a plane
of green spaces where dead leaves are raked up and plants are watered depending on the season
of small screws to be inserted into who knows what component parts
At times like that I understand them intimately but dare not tell them I belong to their caste

To be the boss you've got to act the boss
They at least would have understood

But not my subordinates my holiday camp supervisors
and group leaders

Monday evening at eight-thirty
I'll revel in my position as a line operator answerable to
his own bosses I'll return to the production lines the
conveyor belts that are like so many roads
No doubt thinking of those towns and villages of France
in the factory just as I thought of the factory on the road

There'll be a little of Aragon's conscript in me

'Oh demons demons that you are
Let me drink my fill of these words'

10.

Coming home from my night's labour
It's starting to lighten a little in the distance towards
the east

Six in the morning and eight hours spent at the
crumbed fish factory turning out moulds
Not mould as in fungus
But the cooking equipment sort like fat Lego blocks
made out of plastic with six holes and very malleable
stacked fifty high that need to be unstacked then put on
a production line that never stops
Then the machine fills the moulds with a thick sauce
Beyond that I can't see

My whole being finds it strange adapting to the rhythm
of my eight-hour night shifts

What time do you get up go to bed have a nap eat have a
coffee or a drink
I thought about pushing everything back by twelve
hours
I clock on at nine in the evening so it's like it's nine in
the morning and the rest follows at the relevant
matching hour
Finish work at five in the morning so that's five at night
My arse

My body clock is as lost as I am in this new factory
Sure it's only been two days my automatic pilot settings
haven't yet kicked in but the nights goddamn

'When night returns and I'm all alone and bored I think
of you I'm just a soldier like all the others out there'
To quote Johnny Hallyday singing to his Sylvie from
Germany
At night I'm just a factory soldier dreaming of my wife
asleep so near and yet so far
Of thousands of malleable plastic moulds of me

As for the crumbed fish
I no longer get to feel superior about working with
real fish
It's all frozen stuff here breadcrumbs and herbs
Tasteless and bland

Short point is
It's seven o'clock
It's daytime
I've got to sleep
I don't know if I should make myself a coffee or pour
myself a glass of red
I'll probably hum one of Johnny's slow numbers to
myself as I lie down next to my sleeping wife whom
I won't dare disturb

'The place where time drags on'

11.

Seven months it's been for him on crumbed fish duty
He's twenty
He's had a gutful
Between the relentless ragging he's endured the shitty atmosphere and the nagging monotony of working nights always working and those frozen crumbed fish that just keep coming

In the middle of the night the noise of the machines drops a little
He asks me why I'm at the factory
I answer him as I answer everyone with the simple and magnificent truth
Left everything to marry the woman I love
Got married
The joy of being here
And the factory well everybody's gotta work
A baby coming soon he asks next
As long as you're working you're allowed to hope

He too is getting married soon
Lots to organise
He's panicking a bit but they're getting there

Later I learn from the scraps of words we exchange that I live not far from where his boyfriend works

A few days later I'm lending a hand on another team
Somebody's telling me about his wedding
They wanted to have a civil partnership ceremony but
with the new law it's easier to adopt if they get married

I smile gently

I think about our former justice minister Madame
Taubira who was so right about the fact that some little
queer working in a factory should be able to say that
he's gay
That he has the law on his side
Even if it's harder at home with his parents
And even if he must have been shitting himself and the
ragging must have been really too much
That he should be able to say
They're going to get married

At the end of my shift I take a Perrier from the
soft-drink dispenser
Champagne

12.

It started like this
I hadn't asked for anything but
When one of the bosses on my shift asks me if
I've ever drained tofu
When I see the number of pallets and pallets and more
pallets that I'm going to have to drain on my own and
I know already this job's going to keep me busy the
whole night

Draining tofu

I repeat the words without much conviction
Tonight I'll be draining tofu
I'll be a tofu drainer all night long

I tell myself I'm about to experience a parallel universe
In the already parallel world that is the factory

Let me set the scene
It's two-thirty in the afternoon
I emerge from my 'night time' having gone to bed
around eight in the morning
I have to clock on at eight-thirty this evening and knock
off at five
The temp agency calls me change of plan change of
hours

From seven in the evening to four-thirty in the morning
which when I include a half-hour daily break will give
me a good nine hours of work
I won't be on crumbed fish but on the ready-cooked
meals also produced by my factory

I start working
I'm draining tofu

I say it to myself over and over
Like a mantra
Almost
Like a magic incantation
Sacred
A password
A sort of summing up of the pointlessness of the
existence of the work of the entire world of the factory
I have a laugh

I try motivating myself
Humming along to the tune of the great Charles
Trenet's *There's Happiness*
I think of Shakespeare's famous lines where the world's
a stage and we are but poor players
I feel like I'm in a real-life version of Kamoulox
That absurdist word-based game show
'I'm singing Trenet as I drain my tofu'
'Alas no go back three crumbed fish'

I think about the fact that tofu is disgusting and if there
weren't vegetarians I wouldn't be stuck doing this crazy
tofu job
I come up with spoonerisms that sound pretty good
to me
Tofu drainer
Faux-fur trainer

My actions start to become automatic
Slice
Open twenty-kilo box of tofu
Put packets each weighing about three kilos on my
work station
Slice
Open the packets
Stand tofu upright on a sort of flat stainless steel
strainer and allow briny liquid to drip through
Let tofu drain for a while

A while
Just like the gag of catchphrase comic Fernand Raynaud
How long does it take for a cannon to cool down
A while
Who still remembers him
Fernand Raynaud and his sketches that seem so tired now
I try to recall them as the tofu drains
Number 22 in Asnières
The Lilac Shirt
Why Are You Coughing
The Cannon Barrel

I remember how my grandmother adored showing them
to me on the TV when I was a kid
I think about her and how much I miss her
I remember
I remember Georges Perec
Hardly surprising

I'm draining tofu
Once the tofu has drained
I put it into a vat cover it with cling wrap put it in a
corner of the workroom where it'll sit before it's
included in who knows what sort of ready-cooked dish
That part's not in my job description

From time to time
I get to use the forklift to take the large bags where I put
my empty boxes and plastic packets to the bins outside
That's good that part
Going out to the bins
Changes it up

Not long ago
In my old factory
I was unpacking chimeras
That was more exhausting though I have to say

Tofu drainer
If you've never drained tofu for nine hours a night you'll
never understand
But shit
Old schmuck that I am I do know and you don't

And there's no glory whatsoever to be had in that
No contempt for the white collars

Contempt
Which brings to mind Godard's masterpiece and I try to
recall Camille's Theme from Georges Delerue's film score
Music that would work well I think here in this
atmosphere
That would work so well
But I can't seem to remember it
Silenzio

The hours go by don't go by I'm lost
I'm in a state of ecstatic half-wakefulness of almost
paradoxical sleep like when you're drifting off and your
thoughts are wandering at the whim of your
unconscious
But I'm not dreaming
I'm not having nightmares
I'm not falling asleep
I'm working

I'm draining tofu
I say it to myself over and over
Like a mantra
I try to think of the spoonerism I came up with earlier
but I can no longer remember it
I tell myself you have to have a sacred belief in the pay
that'll wind up leaving you with a love of the absurd or
of literature
In order to keep going

You have to keep going
Draining tofu
Every now and again
Go out to the bins

Break comes at ten past one in the morning
It'll go until twenty to two
I don't know if it's legal to have your break more than
six hours after you start
But I couldn't give a shit
I've still got three hours of draining tofu

Smoke
Coffee
Smoke
A Snickers
Smoke
A text from my wife who was thinking of me at
eleven o'clock
I smile tenderly
If she knew
But time's up
One last drag as if to say
You've seen the factory you've seen the tofu you will not
have my last smoke
My arse
I stub it out quickly

Head back to the locker room quick smart
Work gear on

Time clock
Back to it

I'm draining tofu
Three more hours to get through
Only three hours to get through
You have to keep going
I'm draining tofu
I'm going to keep going
This night is never-ending
I'm draining tofu
This night will never end
I'm draining tofu

I'm draining tofu

13.

It's tough going but you keep a lid on it at the factory

It's the weekend
I've forgotten how to sleep
I should be on my production line at this hour
I should have two more hours of work
Two more hours of crappy work
Of processing
Of being on the line

It's the weekend
I should be regathering my labour power
I mean
Resting
Sleeping
Living
Somewhere other than at the factory
But that bitch of a place
It's devouring me

I've just gone outside at home to have a smoke
The autopilot actions of my night-time breaks come rushing back
Take a drag do it quickly light up the next one from the butt of the first

I'll be back at it the day after tomorrow
It's as if it's

Tomorrow
You start to work on the rhythm of your sleep
The rhythm of life
That's imposed by the factory

You have to go back there
You have to sleep
You have to

This factory is bloody killing me
With its fucked up rhythms
And the insane things you have to do every night

Don't talk about it
Write it

My muscles are killing me
It's killing me too this hour's break I should be having
but I'm not
Smoking my ciggie at home
I'm still at the factory

Who'll be able to give me a lift tomorrow or the day
after
Working nights I'm losing the sense of the days
It's tough

If I can't share a ride I won't have a job
That'll be it
That'll be shit
I'll see what I can sort out with my fellow workers

But that'd mean having to talk to each other
Despite the earplugs the machines that pound away our silences in the break why say anything and anyway what would you say
That it all sucks
That you're struggling to sleep on the weekends
But you're making out
As if
Everything is just fine
You've got a job
Even if it's a shit one
Even if you never get to rest
You're earning a few bucks
And the factory's going to consume us
And is already consuming us

But you don't talk about that
Because at the factory
It's like it goes when Brel sings
'Monsieur
You don't talk about that
You don't talk about that'

14.

You should see our faces
Furrowed
At the break
Features drawn
Fixed gaze lost in the distance in the smoke of our cigarettes
Broken gargoyles
If I dare draw the parallel to the Great War
We
The petty factory soldiers
Waiting to be sent to the front
Or rather
Mercenaries
No longer the year's Marie-Louise conscripts
But
Waves of volunteers in a war against the machine
Fighting a losing battle
Sure
But at least bringing in a monthly wage

The break
That damned break
Longed for dreamed of waited for from the time you clock on
And even if it will be too short anyway
If it comes too soon
There'll be more hours to get through
If it comes too late

You can't take any more can't take any more
It will come

Triumphant capitalism has learned the lesson well that to best exploit the worker
You have to look after them
Just a bit
You make do with what you've got
Rest up for half an hour
Little lemon
There's still some juice left in you that I'm just going to squeeze out

Thirty minutes
That about sums it up
The time clock is obviously either before or after the locker room
Depending on whether you're leaving work or about to start
By which I mean
That's at least four minutes lost
Changing as fast as you can
The time it takes to go to the common room to get a coffee
The corridors the stairs that seem never-ending
Lost time
Dear Marcel I found what you were looking for
Come to the factory and I'll show you quick smart
Lost time
You won't have to spend so long belly-aching about it

And at last some fresh air
At last you're outside
Ciggie
Look at the time on your mobile
Let's make it twenty minutes
The throbbing noise of the factory I find almost soothing
Some shut themselves away in their car
Others eat
From what I can smell there are joints being smoked somewhere in the distance
I'm sitting on a bench and I light up a dark tobacco rollie from the stub of my last one

Look at the time
Think every minute that's passing
Hardly makes up for the time that's lost
Light up another smoke from the butt of the last

Just fifteen minutes more
How much time do I need to get back up
Change
Take a leak
Obviously the boss wouldn't tolerate you going to the crapper in the hour just before or after your break
You'll just have to wait a bit
You should have thought about that beforehand
Alright so I don't really know
But I can imagine

The drags on your smoke become more anxious
The glances at your mobile more frequent
Frenetic
As times passes
No longer making up for anything
Get going
Got to go back

Try to snatch thirty seconds of outside air knowing
you'll have to be even faster in the corridors on the
stairs in the locker room

Last drag on the ciggie
Last glance at the mobile
Got to go back up

I always think of my good mate Apollinaire right at that
moment
I imagine him with his pipe
In the trenches
Just before the whistle blows
Thinking of Lou
As I'm here thinking about my wife
'While with eyes fixed on my watch I await the moment
when we'll go over the top'

15.

There are some nights when everything runs smoothly
When everything runs like the *made in Sweden* forklifts we've been given
I manage to reverse parallel park first go whereas with the old ones I'd always struggle

Even better my colleagues on the previous shift have made up one and a half hours on my production line
So every now and again I can go for a quick wander down the corridors of the factory
Take a little bit longer at the outside bins and even sit down for a break outside for thirty seconds
Glance at my mobile
Lend a hand to my colleagues who haven't been so lucky

The night goes by peacefully
The hours feel gentle
I think of that line I thought came from Ronsard but which is in fact Desportes
'And time so fleet of foot slips by without a trace'

It slips
Like water from a duck's feathers
Like papa into mama

I have a heightened sensation of existing in this world
In almost Spinoza-like accord with my environment
Le Grand Tout that is the factory

I am the factory it is me it is it and I am me

Tonight
We labour

16.

Mohamad calls me at five in the evening
His temp agency has just changed his hours
He's not starting at the same time as me at seven but
with another team on the nine o'clock shift
That's the end of the car-pooling
He's sorry but 'You get the fact I'm not about to wait
outside the factory or do the round trip there and back'
Of course I get that

This I get too
The precarious nature of work
Given the whim of HR who call the agency who wreck
any proletarian attempt at car-pooling or anything else
But on a much deeper level in a more insidious manner

I'll give you an example
You're working nights or you're taking a nap after work
The temp agency calls
Your phone is off
Message there when you wake up
'Your shift starts two hours earlier than usual'
The agency is closed when you try to call to say that you
can't
It's too late
You should already be on the job
Another casual will be replacing you tomorrow

I'm back on crumbed fish
It's five in the evening I'm clocking on in two hours and
I too have just woken from my nap and have just hung
up from Mohamad
The factory is a good fifteen kilometres from home
Anxiety starts to mount just as drops of sweat start
trickling from my armpits
Taxi
It's my only option
Get dressed quick smart
Walk to a rank in town so at least I don't have to pay
the supplement for when they come to pick you up at
your place

Name of the factory
Yes yes he knows it
Radio RTL is broadcasting a debate for the primaries
on the right and is giving oxygen to the candidates who
want to suspend the in-work welfare benefits of violent
demonstrators hey what more people taking advantage
of the system who don't want to work and even better
who are lashing out at law enforcement and
smashing shop windows yes they're definitely on
in-work benefits those guys
Definitely on benefits
Keep my mouth shut so I don't scream
The driver asks if I'm one of the bosses seeing as
I'm taking a cab to the factory
I tell him I'm Agnès Saal's son but he doesn't seem to
get the joke
Soon I'm there

I'm suddenly ashamed
I don't want my co-workers to know I've come in a taxi
I don't know why

Although they do know that I car-pool with Mohamad
But
It's as if by arriving like that I'm making out that
I'm rich
Except that I'm paying my fare with my overdraft
Suppressed shame
Shame of the subjugated
Not wanting to say
Well yeah I've taken a cab 'cos my ride-share dumped
me and I don't want to lose my job

I tell the driver to drop me off five hundred metres away
from the parking lot
I'm hoping not to be seen getting out of that vehicle
Armpits sweaty like they were before
Pay the fare which has got to equate to half a night's
wages
Pay to be paid
Pay so as not to be sacked from a crumbed fish factory
So as not to lose credit with the temp agency
But that's something nobody will ever know
Nobody saw me get out of the cab

Or maybe some people did and they're just pretending
Like I too am pretending

17.

Another change of shifts for Mohamad
Frankly they're just screwing us all around
This evening
I'm skiving

Not taking a taxi two nights running
And anyway it was the last night
Before the weekend
Bugger that for a joke
Exhaustion from the week has caught up with me
The bosses
They can do without me
The factory
It can do without me

I'll come up with some fake excuse when I call up ten
minutes before I'm due to start
I'll be put on to a boss I don't know
The one from the afternoon shift

'Oh la la what a nightmare my car wouldn't start
My canary died
Or my grandmother
Frankly I've had too much of a gutful to be able to be
there this evening
You'll get the message to my boss's team'

I'll call the temp agency right after that and get through to the answering service
That'll be perfect
Same fake message

I see a luminous horizon like a sunset over the island of Houat on a summer's evening
Take a nap
Get up when I feel like it
Shower for half an hour
Cut my nails clean my ears with cotton wool buds snip off a hair the hairs that are sprouting from my moustache put something sweet-smelling under my armpits put in the earring I haven't worn for a month because it's forbidden at the factory
Make myself look good for the return of my wife who will be surprised to see me when she gets home from work

Before that and after my session in the bathroom
Go have a quiet pre-dinner beverage at the local bar at a sensible time
Buy myself a kebab with chips and mayonnaise which I'll eat on our deck

Water our plants and our flowers
Hydrangea jasmine fuchsia honeysuckle
And the others whose names I don't know
Life the real one
Simple pleasures

One beautiful evening and night ahead
Like stolen freedom
It has no price
Not even my night's wages

Tonight
I'm going to flirt with my wife

It'll be beautiful like when I skipped class as a teenager
to go and flirt with the girls in the pretty month of May

Beautiful like when a boss is tearing his hair out
wondering how he's going to keep his production line
running when he's one operator down
That will be his problem
No longer mine
Not this evening
Not tonight

18.

Get back from the factory
One of the first reflexes
A habit to set things to right as soon as you get home
Take off your shoes and the double pair of socks
Let your feet breathe far from the boots and blue plastic booties that you put on inside your boots so as not to pick up anything disgusting from the line operator before you
No regulation boots
With the size written on top
Luckily manage to find a size forty-five pair

Bit of pain in my right foot these last few days
Haven't paid it much attention

Was having a bit of a chat with a co-worker
'I saw the doc yesterday
My toe
A fungal infection'

Take a look at my foot when I get home
The nail on my big toe
Bluish-purple

No need to look further
Three months it's been that my right big toenail has been purple
Three months that I've been at the factory

The damp
The shared boots
Nothing fatal oh no
Just something a little painful and a bit ugly at the end of your foot
It's never going to be a work-related illness
Toe fungus
It's never going to be silicosis

Today I processed béchamel sauce in the mixer in industrial quantities
The proportions were simple
For one 164-litre vat of sauce from which we will make I don't know how many individual potato gratins that will be sold at Monoprix
Add 57 litres of cream
3.66 kilograms of egg yolks
110 litres of water
Mix
Add 30 kilograms of magic powder
Mix

I don't know how many vats I mixed
I imagine the cream would have been better
With mushrooms
The ones from our feet for example

19.

You have to read *Diary of a Labourer* by Thierry Metz
That book is a masterpiece
Published under Gallimard's L'Arpenteur imprint in the 1990s
It was Isabelle Bertin who told me on Facebook I should read that book
Ordered it quick smart like all the books about this working life I can find at the moment
Got it that same day
It's a total smack in the face

Look it up on Google
Thierry committed himself drank then suicided one of his sons having been knocked down by a car and killed
A poet according to the websites
No more than that
I ordered the rest of his works immediately

No more than a sketch
That language
Towards which I'd dearly like to reach
Those words
The silence of work

I quote
'It's Saturday. My hands are idle. You can hear the kids playing on the sand and the cars going past . . .

The chairs chatter away inside the house. About
what who knows. Whatever is said it doesn't matter.
It's just a word that is uttered, a whispering of
old women ... Between two meals, two sets
of dishes.'

The last time I got blown away by something like that
Was in another life reading
Fragmentation of a Shared Place
By Jane Sautière
Such clear-sightedness about an occupation

In another life
I knew Isabelle Bertin and she knew me
I don't know if she knows that

We were in Nancy in the early 2000s
I was studying social work
She was the prof

It was fifteen years ago
I wasn't a fan
I don't know why now
But I didn't like her
I really didn't
Fifteen years later
I don't know if it was from some random friend request
on the internet's great social network perhaps I guess
because of my other book
I'm not writing about social work anymore
But about the factory instead

She acknowledges that
And suggests I read Thierry Metz

Metz Nancy
The history of these places stretches back forever
The Lorraine
Bergamot candies plums at the end of August the
plaque from 1477 in the old town commemorating the
death of Charles the Bold the suburb of Haut-du-Lièvre
or Haudul as the locals know it so altered since the last
time I was there the prison relocated up from the station

The factories in the Lorraine
No agro industry like there is in Brittany
Steelworks
Good and dead
A litany
Florange Gondrange Hayange Hagondange
Pont-à-Mousson and its cast iron manhole covers
walked over by the whole of France
Villerupt and its film festival
Longwy and its borders
Ritals from Italy and Polaks from Poland

Nancy a town so bourgeois and so Tuscan in the spring
time when the cathedral of Saint-Epvre and the
surrounding streets are bathed in sunlight
And Metz so German whose railway station and
platforms were studied prior to 1914 for the unloading
of goods in the event of war

Let me come back to Thierry
His book
Towards the end

Which sums up
More or less
My work at the factory

'At some point it'll be over.
Voilà.
That's all one can say.
Here.'

I hope that reading these words is the ultimate outcome for a teacher
One of her former students expressing his eternal gratitude

Voilà
That's all I could say
Here

20.

'Given the existence as uttered forth in the public works . . .'

As it is for every temp agency throughout France
The eleventh of the month is payday
The eleventh is to the casual worker
What the fifth is to the welfare recipient
What the twenty-eighth of the previous month is to your regular worker

Knowing the crowds who'd be hanging around
I had a book in my pocket
Anticipating the wait
The absurdity of the work we do
I chose *Godot* from the great Sam

In the queue
People play games on their mobiles they wait they smoke they chat about things sometimes all at the same time
I read absentmindedly

Something makes me think of my cousin Camille who has just started the intensive foundations course in humanities in preparation for the *Grandes Écoles*
As did I twenty years ago

On her syllabus
The great classics
Racine Corneille Hugo Genet Proust Céline
Du Bellay La Fontaine
And Beckett who's waiting
Who'll still be waiting
Like the rest of us in the queue
Like Vladimir Estragon Pozzo
And Lucky which I will be if I get my dough

At reception it's the same ritual with the adorable
secretary
Like it is every month
'Hi Joseph you here for your slip'
A smile every time
Uh yeah
It's like going back to school to collect my report
School report or pay slip
Um well I couldn't care less about any report or any slip
I just want my cheque

Had I known
Twenty years earlier
Sitting at the desks of the elite
Supposed
That old man Godot would be helping me laugh about
all this
Twenty years later
About the temp work
About the crumbed fish
About the unspoken report

I have my cheque
I'm off
I stop by the bank
I get my dough

Home again
I sprawl out on the sofa

'Silence. [I] remain motionless, arms dangling,
head sunk, sagging at the knees.'

21.

I remember learning to read
With the good Jesuit brothers who educated me
Using G. Bruno's *A Tour of France with Two Children*
I'll doubtless never know why the priests chose that particular masterpiece for us
So symbolic of the Third Republic
But that's not the point
André and Julien the little orphans from Moselle travelled through France on the lookout for manual labour
Armed with their booklet containing the remarks and appraisals of their previous bosses
I remember history lessons too which looked at the issue of the worker's booklet
The industrial revolution
The inevitable rise of capitalism
Paternalism
The familistery of Guise

These days at the factory
Obviously enough
There are no longer workers' booklets
Where the boss notes down your service record
And you have to show it
To each new boss

However I have been issued with
A notebook

Small format
Fits into the pocket of your work jacket
'New Employee Integration Record'
That's what it's called

Every day
At the end of the job
I have to have it filled in and signed by the supervisor of the production line I've just worked
This goes on for three weeks
The areas for evaluation vary from one week to the next and are assessed like this
Dark green
Excellent
Light green
Satisfactory
Orange
To be improved
Red
Unsatisfactory

Let me list the areas

Week 1
Team spirit
Punctuality
Hygiene
Communication skills
Safety

Week 2
Conduct
Handling non-standard matters
Precision
Respect for rules
Safety

Week 3
Taking initiative
Commitment
Interpersonal skills
Self-control
Safety

It's so we know if everything's going well
And how I can improve my opportunities for promotion
in the organisation
So they say

But watch out if I don't have my little book filled in
every day
And if I don't have it in my coat pocket at all times
The bosses insist
Anybody
Anybody is entitled to ask for my book
At any time

It is the unanimous opinion of every factory worker
Who is not a boss
That it is fucking pointless
Nobody

Nobody has ever been asked to show their book
By anybody

Doesn't stop the fact
I see it more as a symbol
A symbol of a capitalist system that will never manage
to forget its deepest roots
Completely
The all-powerful boss
Wielding the power of life and death over a worker's
career
Like the good old days of the Third Republic
When children were toiling away
In the mines
Or somewhere else

22.

Ten to five in the morning

Bike
Lorient cold a bit misty but not yesterday's dreadful drizzle
It's not Dutronc's song
Almost five
But Lorient in autumn is a bit like Paris
Minus the metro
I'm off jobbing and some party animals are sleeping it off in a bus shelter
Worlds colliding
Hood up pedalling
'Hey Darth Vader you going to some party for Halloween'
Just shut it mate
If only you knew
I'm done with the crumbed fish
Got a week back on prawns

Five twenty-nine

A new casual here since yesterday
Out on the smoker's terrace
Clearly working flat out
Doesn't stop gabbing
It's good unboxing crates of prawns makes me feel like
I'm at rugby training I play number 8 for Lanester and

at our last training I lost a tooth I'm seeing the dentist
on 19 November who do I tell around here that I won't
be coming in that day
You're in luck the boss is right over there
The boss drinks his coffee smokes his ciggie and
answers
'You can come see me in the office and tell me there
didn't you only start yesterday and your hot date it's the
19th of November right you can leave off telling me for
a couple of weeks'

Seven hours and barrow loads

I'm unboxing crates and crates of twenty kilos of frozen
prawns before they go off to be cooked
Almost enjoying the physical labour
I'm on autopilot

Nine thirty-two

Take a break outside
View out over the sand quarry next to the factory
Some lingering dew drops
It's almost pretty
Be content with what you have
The River Blavet's there in the distance with a few sails
hanging out for the Atlantic as much as I'm not hanging
out to get back to work
I have another quick coffee on the smokers' terrace
The new casual has been spiked by a frozen prawn this
morning

Shit luck must be said because of the risk of pruritus
and the subsequent drama if you don't look after it

Time unknown

On sorting prawns post-cooking
Far and away my favourite job
Contemplative
Monastic
Stoic
Mystical almost

I watch the prawns being sorted on a conveyor after
being cooked
Parading past at a rate of three tonnes an hour
I'm doing the maths as I watch
That's one and a half tonnes every half-hour
That's seven hundred and fifty kilos every quarter of an
hour
That's two hundred and fifty kilos every five minutes
I watch fifty kilos of prawns go past every minute

Nothing happens except for a few broken prawn heads
that go into the relevant container
Prawns keep going past more and more of them
I'm in a corner my back to the factory floor pretty close
to the wall
And I get to stuff my face as long as I keep a bit of an eye
out for the bosses who come by every now and then
Prawns go by just as the time does

Apart from that
As expected ahead of autumn and the coming festive season
We're finally getting into crustaceans shellfish and other fun stuff
Whelks
Scampi
Crab claws
We cook them

The whelks are clearly no longer of any interest

The scampi have no taste and no texture so they're disgusting

As for the crab claws we had a hard time until yesterday working out how to try them on the sly
It was Fabrice who figured out a way
A metal door into one of the storerooms
Open the door
Insert the claw into the opening
Close it gently but firmly making sure the bosses don't hear
We took turns having a taste
Nothing of interest except that it was forbidden

We'll see when it gets to lobster time
Even if I doubt it'll be as good
As the time it is now
Knock-off time

One minute past three

Back in the locker room
They've opened up the new bloke's hand with a sterilised Stanley knife and applied some Dakin's solution
Pulled out the splinter of prawn that was still in there with a pair of tweezers

Ten past three

Back on the bike
Just over half an hour and I'm home
If I go easy on the pedals
It's still less than an hour
Tops

23.

I was supposed to take on a long job on Monday
Two months on whelks
The most bloody pointless shellfish in the world
Two months of work

It's delayed by a week
Machines not yet run in

It's Friday and it's raining the way it only can in Brittany
I won't be clocking on at three in the morning on
Monday as if I were over the moon
At taking my bike in the Breton rain when most people
are asleep

Of course on the phone I put on a good face when the
temp agency called
Despite the 'Oh fuck really' that slipped out

The weekend doesn't feel the same
It's not the calm before the storm
There won't be tonnes of whelks to process on Monday
for two months' guaranteed work
No hours to count on next week

I don't know if it's raining in Nantes
But it's raining in Lorient
And
My heart is aching

24.

It's been two weeks on whelks already and I still don't
know which end of these god-awful shellfish
I'm meant to pick up
Do I shovel them
The old-fashioned way
And go with the wretchedness
Or snatch them haphazardly
From the conveyor
And waft along with my wandering thoughts

The processing area is at the start of the production line
and must measure two hundred square metres
Three doors
One leading out to the corridor of the factory where the
Pal-Boxes are brought in
Crates of five hundred kilos of frozen whelks to be
stuffed into the cooker
A second leading out to said whelk-cooking processing
line
And another that's hardly ever used leading out to the
prawn processing line

When we clock on at three
There are three of us
Line supervisor
Cooker
And casual

We set up
We do the prep
We work out how behind they got the day before
We get stuck in
The whelk processing line is new so nothing's really
organised nothing's working properly

My job is to shovel the whelks into the huge metal belly
where they'll be cooked
There's no equipment
I do it with a spade

This afternoon I was discussing it with my hairdresser
and tried explaining it to her
The almond shampoo smelled so good in my hair
instead of that dead shellfish smell

'But it's a new factory'
'Yeah, well, your salon is new too but if you don't have
clippers and only scissors and a shaver from the fifties
you're not going to do the same job with shitty rollers
and all the stuff from back then'

And suddenly she stops
'Oh yeah bloody hell'

When the supervisors aren't there
We all say the same thing
It's just the same old same old
Always wanting to rush things through
Nothing good ever comes of it

And soon it will be Christmas and the holiday season
And the machines don't work

Boss
Why don't you come out of your office and pick up a shovel for five minutes down here on the shop floor and you'll see how much faster a forklift would be

Recurrent refrains
Those slogging
Those bossing
Production line rhythms proclaimed from on high

The reinforcement arrives at four-thirty
A good bloke who works hard
A casual
The rugby player who'd spiked himself with a prawn
He seems passionate about the whelk processing line

When he clocked on
'Hey d'you see the team from yesterday arvo they were five Pal-Boxes down on their quota but not us'

Man
A good guy but really
It's like it's his factory his production line like they're his whelks
For a casual like me
Nothing's going to change
Whether things run well or not
So just go and pick up your shovel mate

Or go beg somebody somewhere for a forklift that will make our life easier for an hour or two
But shut up
It's early
Too early

We go at it together
One with a shovel emptying the Pal-Boxes into the machine
The other running the show
Bringing in the pallets
Slicing them open with the Stanley knife
Unboxing them
Lining them up
Opening them
Cutting them open again
Unstacking them
We alternate every two hours or so

At the start of the day
It takes me barely a quarter of an hour to empty a five-hundred-kilo Pal-Box with a shovel
At the end
It's a good half-hour at least

Four hours of shovelling
Break
Another four hours of shovelling
Finish

And the stench of those first days
That stench of whelk
Of dead rat of sludge of piss and bad wine
Mixed
Macerated
Soaked
I don't even notice it anymore

When I started on whelks
I didn't think I could stick it out
But it's getting better now
You tell yourself you're getting used to it
Soon it will already have been two weeks

One of my aunts dropped by our place the day before
yesterday an hour or two after knock-off
I was eating reheated sauerkraut from the weekend
with a glass of white
We chat about the factory for a bit
We have a drink
My eyes must look a bit dry and slow to focus and I'm
struggling for words
I try to say
I'm fighting for words much as my body battles at work

'But I suppose it's not something you can really describe
is it' she says to me

Silence
I pour us another glass

25.

'We must labour in order to render ourselves most worthy of some position: the rest does not concern us, it is a matter for others'

Jean de la Bruyère
The Characters

End of the day
'You don't have a smoke' he asks me 'my wife left this morning with the car and the wallet'
I hold out my packet of tobacco
'Ah they're rollies great won't bother you then if I take two or three so it'll see me through until this evening when she gets back'

The next day
He's paired up with me
My usual co-worker is away

Since clocking on at three in the morning until I don't know what time
And despite the stench of the factory to which my nostrils have nonetheless grown accustomed
He is reeking of alcohol and red-eyed
He's irritated his gestures jerky

Partied hard I think to myself
Or a rough night

Our break falls at the same time
I ask him for a smoke
'Ah well no you see in fact my wife like she didn't come
back so that's that then'

He quickly changes the subject
Says loud and clear he was a deep-sea fisherman before
Then an accident and so on his back is shattered shows
me photos of x-rays of his spine on his smartphone
Colleagues come over
Deep-sea fisherman
Magical words
He talks of port visits to the Ivory Coast to Chile and the
islands
I chew on my tobacco

The next day
I'm partnered with him again
He's jawing away on some gum
Perhaps yesterday the alcohol was masking his boorish
incompetence
He's slack
He's ineffective
Kicks into gear the minute a figure appears
On the shop floor where we work
One person loads up the conveyor belt with whelks
using muscle power and a shovel
The other manages supplies boxes pallets bins and the
rest of it

To begin with he's loading whelks
Doesn't seem to matter how much I tell him
Easy
Careful
Steady
That he has to load up the belt at a regular rhythm
No stopping and starting steady but persistent so the
whelks are uniformly spread out

Every fifteen minutes he clocks the time
'Hey we'll be done soon'

Two hours later it's no use
Still gaps
Weird and wonderful bizarre hillocks of shellfish

He covets my work longingly and I can see in his eyes
that he thinks that I've got it pretty good swanning
around the factory with a forklift or some bins

'Hey we'll be done soon
I'm going home to pour myself a fat shot of rum straight
up rum's good it is like when I was in the West Indies'

The boss arrives
Yells about the conveyor belt of whelks
Full of uneven holes

I grumble

When he leaves we change jobs
I take the shovel
My workmate smiles
He gets the forklift

It's not long before the pallets of whelks on the side
start to run low
The empty boxes and rubbish bins build up
He curses the forklift that's not running smoothly
The Stanley knife that's not cutting cleanly
Punches the wall
Sulks for a moment

The boss reappears
'What the hell's this pigsty I don't care what you have to
do to get this place ship-shape just do it there's no way
this is gonna continue with your stuffing around'

It's at this moment exactly
When the boss nicks off and my workmate rediscovers
his I-couldn't-give-a-fuck attitude that I feel like
Smacking him in the face with my spade
Sliding a banana peel under the forklift
A swig of frozen whelks down his back
And other such pleasantries

I don't feel like losing my job because of some
incompetent full-of-shit alcoholic
I'm dying to go see the boss and tell him on the quiet
'Eh you do know it's bozo over there and not me'

Another break that falls at the same time as his
I retreat outside and return only for a last coffee before
having to start again
'Where were you then mate
You don't have a smoke do you'

Skiving
I hear him saying to another bloke a bit further on
'Oh yeah you know pay comes in this arvo first thing I'm
gonna do is go straight to buy some smokes'

The day's irritation passes
I look back over my pre-factory working life
How many colleagues covered up my incompetence my
drunkenness or my infuriating habits
Without making a fuss about it
Without saying a thing about it
Without ever referring it to the boss
How many colleagues did I manage to piss off
Justifiably
With my arrogance my laziness my utter hopelessness
Or with whatever else that I'll never know
Since they never said a thing

Why is it he irritates me so much and others don't yet
they're just as dumb
Criticism being nothing more than projection
He must be me this workmate
Or so I fear
An image of my darker side
I'm convinced of it

In other words
There's truth in what the old fellow says
La Bruyère that is

'Those who, knowing us insufficiently, think poorly of us do us no wrong: it is not us they criticise, but a creation of their own imagination.'

Doesn't stop the fact that today again
He was bumming smokes

26.

My offsider
He's in mighty fine form today
Hopping about like a mad flea
Clearly his wife has returned
Yesterday he was telling me he was expecting to engage
in some 'bedroom sports'
This morning he's having a laugh
He's telling jokes you'd expect from some young bloke
and in such good taste

'A black guy and a white guy are pissing from a bridge
The white guy says – it's a cool breeze
The black guy replies – water's pretty cool too'

He howls with laughter for a good minute

Later
Still all smiles

'Bloody hell mate you should've seen
The tub of yoghurt I delivered to her
She wouldn't have believed it was possible
If she didn't already know me and my tackle
A goddamned tub of yoghurt it was'

Later
He's singing *La bohème* at the top of his lungs for an hour
La bohèèèèèèème

Later still

‘When I get home
I’m going to arse-fuck her straight up
She’s going to be howling
I promise you’

At one point
He howls as much as he’d like to hear her howl

‘She’s gonna hoooooooooowl’

He has the eyes of a lunatic

Later still
A female colleague comes onto the shop floor
She’ll be providing an extra pair of hands over the
holiday period so she thought she’d introduce herself
He makes his cute little puppy-dog eyes
‘I used to be a deep-sea fisherman’

I disappear off to look for a pallet of whelks

When I get back
She’s no longer there
And he’s straight back into it

‘D’ya see that little thing
Just asking to be laid straight on the table
And have her pussy cracked wide open

That's the good stuff right there
Crrr-aaaa-ckkkk her pussy wide open'

Stunned
I don't know what to say except that
My wife is perfect
Pause
Same crazy eyes as before

'Ah yes that's true mine too
So what'

A sordid oily laugh rises from the shop floor and chills me more than the tonnes of frozen whelks I've been working with for weeks

Later still
He comes over to me again

'What does your wife do then'
'Teaches disadvantaged girls'
'Oh, that's cool that is
That's a decent profession
I'd really like to have done that
Teach disadvantaged girls'

He is deadly serious when he utters those words

27.

Life is a shit sandwich and every day you bite off another mouthful
As my grandmother would philosophise on the not so good days

It's wrong
Shit is a sandwich of whelks that you have to unload by the pallet when one section of the conveyor belt in a production line breaks down

If that isn't the hell
Which you can bet is coming your way
It's a bitch of a shit-filled purgatory

A purgatory of pain caused by the random positions
I adopt in an effort to manage without that goddamned conveyor belt

The maw of the machine claims its unrelenting share of whelks
I compensate for the belt
I am the link

Processing must continue

The bosses know but can't do a thing
Not a single one has been sighted in our processing area since it broke down yesterday

The mechanics are at a loss
A part has been ordered but they're not even certain that'll fix it
It'll happen at some point
Nobody knows when
It'll happen and in the meantime our spines are breaking our lower backs are screaming our arms are being wrenched apart

Yesterday I reached the point where I was singlehandedly loading ten-kilo bags of whelks into a hole in the machine as if I was trying to sink a basketball through the hoop
Just trying to find a physically workable solution
Completely dumbass
But
When you no longer know what to do
Don't know how to relieve one part of your body
You load up some other part and tell yourself the new pain can't get any worse

Processing must continue

The constant pain
The pointlessness of it all
And all this for whelks that will never stop coming

The fact you can see your colleagues in the distance bringing in yet more pallets
Whelks slipping into the gaping mouth of the cooker
Slowly

Almost methodically
Inexorably

Those who have survived a near-death experience swear
to having passed through a long tunnel of blinding
white light
But I can promise you purgatory is there at the mouth
of the tunnel cooker on a whelk processing line

So why continue
To process something about which I don't give a shit
To test my limits
To tell myself that a whelk will not break my skin my
arms my back and above all else it will not break my
mind
It is the grey matter in my brain that is resisting
That will resist

And even if it's only Wednesday and it will truly be hell
this coming Saturday when I'll have worked
The factory will be my Mediterranean across which I'll
map the perilous routes of my Odyssey
The prawns my sirens
The whelks my Cyclops
The broken conveyor yet one more storm

Processing must continue

Dreaming of Ithaca
Notwithstanding the shit

28.

I had never eaten
Crayfish or king crabs from Kamchatka

Nor whelks for that matter
There were some pretty exotic things being cooked at the time
Coming into Christmas
Shellfish for the rich
By the tonne upon tonne

Working six days out of seven for three weeks on the night shift
I consider myself entitled to eat my fill at my place of work
And to take home as much as my pockets can hold

Until now it's been a spot of
Artisanal misappropriation
Two crayfish here
A crab claw there
But now
It's going to get serious

I may only be a small-time worker
All good

I've worked out the technique
I've got the schedules the hiding places and the methods
for getting the stuff out

Two crayfish then
Freshly cooked back home yesterday with some warm
basmati rice and homemade mayo
Crayfish isn't so bad

I'm not stealing anything
It's nothing more than some working-class
reappropriation
Everybody does it

Given the hours we work
Six days out of seven
Given the work we get through
Given the daily bonuses the bosses give themselves
according to the tonnage processed by the little line
operators
Given the margins made by the company on the final
retail price
I'm not going to take two measly crayfish and some
Kamchatka king crab

That crab is crazy
Outlandish legs an invasive species with no predator to
prey on it in those cold waters over there
And goddamn it's good
And fuck it's expensive

I'm reclaiming my factory
My own way
For Christmas which is coming
If I could
I'd take two crayfish per person
And an endless supply of crab legs

At night on my production line
I dream
Of meals washed down with champagne from my hometown
With the people I love
Lots of people
Eating
Laughing
Drinking
Smoking
With a fireplace and a fir tree
Listening to *Christmas Carols* on Radio FIP like so many Christmas songs
Playing a game of tarot with the last ones standing
Eating little crayfish and crab sandwiches and revelling in a 'guard against' bid in the tarot hand

It helps me to hang in there
These hellish bloody six days out of seven
At least one more six-day week
I'll be at it on Saturday 24 December
And who knows what other days

I'm already weeping at the thought of the pent-up
exhaustion
I'm laughing at the absurdity and the whelks
I'm hoping
For crayfish from the Caribbean
Where the water is so warm you can swim comfortably
every day
For king crabs from faraway Kamchatka so far
Away
Peninsula of freezing seas
Not far from Japan and Alaska
Where fanciful crabs abound

29.

'You're done
See you later'
That's what the boss said at the end of the day
Just like that no explanation

Six weeks spent together on the shellfish and crustacean shift with
The winkles
The whelks
The king crabs
The crayfish
The scampi
Isn't going to change my status as a casual

Six weeks
And I'm not even sure he knows my first name
A handshake morning and night and his thin smile when he sees I've turned up
With my spade
To be paid

You're done
One 27th of December
Having started on shellfish
One 14th of November

You're done
Done clocking on at half past midnight

Six days out of seven
With the equipment packing up on day three of the job
Done doing whatever it takes just to get through feeling barely human
With whelks falling into your boots that bother you more than any scruples you might have
Done with the stench you can no longer smell

Done with the fury of the ten supervisors who show up one 21st of December when the crayfish aren't being packed as fast as they'd like
Done with wondering why they leave three hours later all smiles even though the production line is moving even slower
And for those three hours feeling the crazy pressure the total stress the cold trickle of sweat as twenty supervisors' eyes scrutinise your every move and the anxiety of stuffing up a forklift manoeuvre of mishandling a simple turn of the shovel

You're done
With the tonnes of whelks to sort and process according to the following order of priority on my production line
Washed whelks
Live whelks
Frozen whelks

You're done
This 23rd of December
A night of whelk-ish apocalypse
It's over five weeks we've been at it

Six days out of seven
Rumours at the factory during the week had been
crazy
Contradictory
Would we have to work on Saturday the 24th
A Christmas truce
First yes
Then no

On the morning of the night of the 23rd people say that
if we process fifteen tonnes of whelks that day
We'll get our Saturday
But they're only rumours
There's an unspoken agreement between our team of
three
Rather a break than a day of pay
Rather think of kin than our coin
So we get stuck in
Fire in our bellies
Beyond exhaustion
We're going for it
We rage against the slightest stoppage of the conveyor
belt
We're not even going to rely on the next team to finish
the job
We all shorten our break by fifteen minutes
We know that perhaps it's in vain and tomorrow we
might have to return
We know that maybe we're being conned by the boss
and maybe anyway we'll get our Saturday
But we don't give a shit

More than thirteen tonnes out of fifteen
The three of us have processed more than thirteen
tonnes of whelks in eight hours
We have a laugh
High fives all round
Hugs all round

'See you Monday'
Says the boss

We won the war of the whelks and the war against
ourselves one Friday 23 December 2016
Those two days of Christmas will be the most precious
thing in the world
And the fastest
Hardly time to eat Sunday lunch with the family
Before I'm back there after coffee
Having to clock on the next day so early

You're done
See you later
Little casual
There wasn't too much bawling out
You weren't off sick
Or worse a workplace accident
The production line never stopped

See you later
That's it for the factory

See you later
That's it for the dosh

Money earned by scrubbing and shovelling with arms and back and gritted teeth and circles under bloodshot eyes and permanently rough and callused hands and your head your head that has to work just to keep you there goddamn it

See you later

Already I can almost hardly wait to
Get back to the factory
As if
I hadn't yet been
To the far end of what's possible to the limit of my exhaustion
To the end of the job
To the end of my work on the factory and myself

'You're done
See you later'
That's what the boss said
There's one of them at last

It's not bosses we're short of
It's jobs
It's money

As long as there is casual work
It'll never be done

There'll be no full stop
I'll have to go back
To start a new line

30.

My wife my love

When you read these words
I will doubtless be in bed
Sprawled
Dreaming of who knows what escapade

You will come home
Finding the house
Tidied the way I do it

The computer with its keypad that was ravaged today
by the paws of the pup you gave me for Christmas and
which we went to choose from animal welfare

I feel like D'Artagnan
I can't remember now if it's at the start of *Twenty Years
After* or in *Bragelonne*
Waiting for a new mission
Brooding
Champing at the bit in the corridors of the Louvre
Like me here at home in Lorient
No work

Waiting for a job

And I'm going stir-crazy
Like a dog

And I'm weeping
At these fucked-up days
With no work
No factory

Today
I saw on the unemployment agency's site

An ad to be an instructor on a sailing boat
Obviously I applied

I relied on my experience with the prawns and fish

Even if it's pointless

I'm hoping to get work
On that boat or at the factory
To bring in some bucks

I'm waiting for work
I'm waiting for the boat to cast off or to dock

I'm waiting for you

PART TWO

'There are no possible words.
It is unimaginable.
But the sun is out. I'm thinking of you'

Guillaume Apollinaire
(letter to Madeleine Pagès, 15 March 1916)

31.

To the slaughterhouse
I go as you would
To be slaughtered

It is perhaps the end point the paradigm the summa
the symbol all that and more of what it can be
The food processing industry

And yet
All I'm doing is cleaning a pig carcass cutting room at
night
The place where I imagine the butchers take over after
the slaughterers have done their work

Now the fish and whelks and ready-cooked dishes and
everything else from before seem inoffensive cute
enough sweet as can be
Even if the work was hard

I have to clean a cutting production line
There's nothing but scraps left from the job done that
day by the workers
I arrive with my hose
Everything is red with blood and white with fat
I give it a preliminary hose-down
A co-worker applies the foam to wash it
I rinse
Another person applies the product that washes it

a second time and doesn't foam up but means we have
to wear gas masks because of the smell and toxicity
I re-rinse
We apply the finishing touches
We tidy up
Job done

The agency called on Monday at four-thirty in the
afternoon for a job that same evening at eight o'clock

Same as the other processing plants
Nobody gives a damn who I am
Two arms that's it
I've never held an industrial cleaning hose
I don't even know how to clean up at home
They couldn't care less

The plant is immense
Monstrously so

A supervisor says
'Pig cutting room'
And I follow him

The door opens
And
The cutting room seems as big as one of my entire
previous processing plants
Blood
Everywhere

It's the first thing
The blood

My eyes try to work out the layout of the workroom and its sections
And then
The scraps of pig
Everywhere
And not just scraps
Snouts spare ribs trotters and the fat so typical of pigs
It's everywhere

I tell myself
What else were you expecting old boy
They made it pretty clear you'd be cleaning an abattoir

The supervisor hands me a hose
Shows me the end of the production line
And tells me
'That's your area
So a guy can come through in two hours' time with the foam'

I turn on the hose
The thing is a nightmare
I do my best
Try to work as quickly and as thoroughly as I can
The boss comes back through
Clearly I'm doing a shit job

I'm guzzling blood
Literally
Can taste it in my mouth
Pigs' blood
Splatter and back spray from the high-pressure jet

At the break in the locker room
Mirrors often frequented and well used
Everybody checks themselves out and washes in silence
My fellow cleaners talk about how in the sections
they've been working
The day shift didn't even clean up their shit
I work out from the thread of their conversation that
they clean the area where the animals are held before
they're killed and the shit they're talking about is not
metaphorical
I count myself lucky with my pigs' blood

I always think I've done a good job cleaning
But it's never good enough
The boss points out a bit of translucent fat about as big
as half a bacon strip stuck in some machinery behind a
metal sheet

The doors open
I see
Hundreds and hundreds of hanging pigs
Pigs carved up every which way into every possible
shape
And a thousand other things that haunt me when I close
my eyes

Patient and resolute my workmates demonstrate the task to me
Me the one incapable of housework
They offer comradely assistance when the boss isn't there

When it's done
I return to the locker room
Wash my face again
Roll some smokes in the endless corridor that takes you out of the factory
Get back in the car
Put on the stereo with the bass turned up playing tunes like *Meat* by Mon Dragon *Harbour City* by Taulard or *Correspondence* by Pour X Raisons
I drive through the night back to my wife who's asleep
The pup wakes up and is all excitement as he welcomes me home
He sniffs me all over
I take him out for a walk
I have treats in my pocket if he does his business outside
It's four in the morning
The town is asleep
He does his business and earns his little pieces of processed frankfurter
I'm hungry and treat myself to the last piece of sausage

In under an hour the slaughterers will be clocking on
I'll have returned to my wife
And started my night

32.

'Dear God! What a lovely thing is war'
That's what he wrote
Apollinaire
From deep in his trench

Trench cleaner
Abattoir cleaner
It's all much of a muchness
It's as if I'm at war
The scraps the fragments the equipment you need the blood
The blood the blood the blood

I'm advancing now
I've moved on from pork to beef
Almost at the front line
Or worse
In the heart of enemy lines

In the 'waste' area
Just half a floor below the slaughter hall
Which means
I clean up all the scraps of cow that can't be used which are then tossed from half a floor up into enormous pipes and into enormous vats which I then clean with my high-pressure hose

As many vats as there are different types of waste
Items I could never hope to identify
Jaws
Horns
Front hooves
Back hooves
Soft furry ears which from time to time still bear the animal's identification tag
Other parts of the body still dripping which I prefer not to think about but which clearly belong to a ruminant beast
Doubtless the different paunches
And udders

I have to use the high-pressure hose to clean out the inside of all the pipes quickly and thoroughly
Then I apply the cleaning foam before hosing it down again and rinsing it off

The walls
The floor

Sometimes the scraps that had been blocking the pipes fall away under the pressure from the hose
And there's an avalanche of above-mentioned bits that tumble down
And they make a big shploooooork
And they make a big splaaaaaaaaash

Mind you don't find yourself under the pipe when the hooves fall

The horns are like so many huge knucklebones strewn over the factory floor
And the udders
Fuck the udders
Like tiny little rugby balls still swollen and body warm from the freshly killed animal
Sometimes they explode when they fall to the ground
A whitish liquid runs out
Stinking of death of the slaughtered creature's bitter stench of fear
It's still warm

I clean up shit too in a purpose-built workroom
I imagine what it's like up above
In 'the trap' as it's known
Where the cattle are taken to wait just before they go through
They're scared and they can smell death approaching
They shit themselves
As you'd expect
I clean it up
It's my job
The job that so horrified me when I heard it described during my break just last week

Three nights now I've been doing it
The first night was horrific
But it's getting easier
You get used to it even if objectively speaking the udders are just as rank just as revolting
And they're still warm from the animal's body

And they stink when they explode
And

And my workmates are good guys
Always there to lend a hand
And at least I have work again through to Friday
That's the main thing

And apparently the abattoir pays well
We'll see soon enough
And you can get used to anything
That's how it is

And I want to believe that my war is lovely
Half a floor below the slaughter hall
Cleaning up the shit and the udders

33.

I remember the footballer Raymond Kopa's severed
fingers when I shook his hand a number of years ago now
It was at the Christmas market in the main square of my
hometown of Reims amid the demountable huts
offering champagne mustard sweets from the region
Or ocarinas crystal monkeys churros and Brazilian
bracelets the same as they do everywhere else

The great Raymond was downing some bubbles looking
fit as a fiddle at the Stade de Reims football club's hut
It took me a few seconds to recognise him
'Monsieur Kopa may I shake your hand'
'Of course young fellow'

I remember his handshake and that some of his fingers
were missing
A kid brought up in the mythology of the great football
club
I thought to myself 'Oh of course he was in the mines
when he was young and the accident when he was
sixteen' along with everything else that people used to
go on about
Roger Marche Wild Boar of the Ardennes
Dominique Colonna who took up at the tobacconist's
on Rue de Vesle
Francis Méano cut down in a car crash and the stand
named after him at the August Delaune stadium where
we'd go if we had any money so as not to be standing in

general admission in the bends of the old velodrome
And Kopa and his accident when he was a kid down the mine

Back at home
I shouted
'Mum mum I saw Kopa I even got to shake his hand'

Fifty years on and Kopa's exploits were still selling dreams

At the abattoir where I work
I shake
Hands that have been sliced
In the locker room
I see
Wooden legs
That blokes slip on before putting on their work coat and their chain mail protective gear

This week
They gave me a new job

I'm no longer cleaning the bovine shit the paunches the horns the blood the fat the death because with my bad eyes and my glasses my sight was too bad and I was leaving too much waste behind

I'm shifting carcasses hanging up on rails
Physical labour
They're quarters of steer or cow or bull or vealer

About one hundred kilos a quarter
I push the carcasses eight at a time
I'm like a rugby prop gesticulating like a station master
shunting his carcasses and guiding them pushing them
towards the lines for 'supermarket orders' 'de-boning'
'ready-to-cut portions' or other sidings

I copped a carcass on my safety boot
When it derailed after I didn't fix my switch plate
My left foot is black and purple despite my steel-toed
overshoe
Lucky I was wearing it because if not the sharp edge
of the carcass would have crippled me

I ask the supervisor how long this job will last
He answers me
'For as long as you're good'

Despite the severed fingers
The wooden legs
The foot I almost lost
The abattoir is selling dreams

And Kopa kicks a ball around when he gets home from
the mine
And I try to write the way Kopa kicked his football
Go Raymond
I drink a glass at the amputees' bar for workers miners
and butchers
Here's to your severed fingers
To Cendrars' severed hand

To Apollinaire's trepanned skull
To my foot saved by a metal toe cap

34.

'You do something else before coming to the abattoir'
'Uh, yeah
Teacher
Social work
All that stuff
Then I guess I left Paris
Married the woman who was waiting for me
Then well I had to do something
And you'
'Yeah pretty much the same
Was in the army
I quit to be closer to my wife
And here I am'

Miniscule parallel lives

Beyond making fun of the military guy who ends up a butcher
Would the reverse be any worse
I don't laugh for long
We're pushing the carcasses of dead beasts

Does he miss his deployments abroad
Does he see the children of Sarajevo or Kigali when he looks at those dead animals
Is he happier in the peace and quiet here not far from the sea with his wife
Just pushing so many dead creatures

Pushing my carcasses
Of course I think back on all those kids full of life whom
I taught who are now adults
Some are dead too
But I'm happy here
With my wife
More than happy
Not far from the sea
Ready to haul dead animals
We're pushing our carcasses
When all's said and done everyone is just lugging their
carcasses

35.

Incessant nightmares hammering
Repetitive
Daily

Not a nap not a night that is free of these nightmares of carcasses
Of dead animals
Tracking me
Attacking me
Violently
Taking on the features of my loved ones of my deepest fears

Endless lifeless nightless nightmares
Starting to wakefulness
Sheets drenched in sweat
Almost every night

Sometimes I scream
Every night I know the slaughterhouse will follow me into my nightmares
And yet
Pushing my quarters of meat each one weighing one hundred kilos
I don't think I'm the worst off

Of what do they dream
The offal workers

Who
Every nap
Every night
Every working day at the slaughterhouse
Watch the heads of cows fall from the floor above
And pick each head up one by one
Fixing it to a suitable piece of machinery between steel hooks
Cutting off cheeks and chops and tossing away the jaws and remains of the skull
Eight hours a day tête-à-tête

Of what do they dream
The leathers guys
That's what they call them the ones who tear off the skins of the animals right after they've been killed
The skins will then be sold to tanners or to god knows who else
They say it's back-breaking that job
That the casuals turn over like the sails of a windmill on a stormy day
That's how hard it is
Physically
Morally
All day
Tearing off cows' skin

Of what do they dream
The guys wielding the branding irons

Because every quarter of every beast is branded with
a slaughterhouse number
A unique identifier
Traceability
They brand the flesh of the animal after the leathers
guys have done their work
Change numbers for every beast
Well yeah
It's one of the jobs in the factory
Some people spend their working day branding the
animals with a branding iron and changing the settings
between each kill

Next week
I've got a date with the physio
My body is being slowly ravaged by this solid month
on carcasses
My whole body
My muscles my joints my lumbar region my cervical
vertebrae
Other body parts that I can't even identify

'The body is a tomb for the soul'
So the ancient Greek maxim goes
And I see that
The soul too can be a tomb for bodies

My nightmares exist just at the point
Of what my body can endure

36.

There are some jokes
They make you laugh all day long
They even make your day
Especially if it's a beautiful day

It's Friday
The start of spring
At knock-off time at noon it's a grand day outside
I'm still laughing like a fool

Clocking on at five am the boss says
'In ten minutes you're changing station so you can be trained up for where you'll be next week'
That means there'll be one more week's work at least
More cash coming in

So a new fridge upstream on the line
The animals are not yet quartered
But have been halved lengthwise
Twenty-four rails of thirty animals each about four hundred kilos
Two hundred and ninety tonnes easy

The animals have to be brought out one by one so they can be sawn and cut into quarters
Nothing to think about
Even less than usual

Just have to keep dragging like a draught horse
Even more than usual

I push five lots of five beasts at a time
Works out at about two good tonnes a go
The toughest thing is getting them past the bends
running from the side rails to the main rail
At the end of which is where the cutters work
You always have to make sure they have a supply of
animals so they don't have to go off looking for their
shit

And most importantly
Most important
Do not forget to remove the hanger steak from inside
each animal so it can be put into a tub that a bloke
comes to fetch every half-hour
I love hanger steak
The 'butcher's cut' as it's known
A muscle from the cow's diaphragm
Just one
Long fibres
Tasty
And costs a bomb

I'm on my own in my huge fridge
Calm and determined
I'm hard at it dragging like a madman
I'm tearing off my hanger steaks
And I'm laughing laughing laughing

The boss comes by to see me
'All good with the new job'
'Yeah boss yeah
But there is one thing
I've just worked out why
There's a shit tonne more blood on the floor in my new fridge than there was in the others'
'Yeah really'
'The steaks are higher'

37.

An ordinary day
Like so many others
Like every day almost
Without those micro-events that get retold
A different shop floor a colleague's smart remark
tomorrow's match or tomorrow's election

Trying to recount what doesn't deserve to be retold
Work stripped back to its barest banality
Repetitive
Simple actions
Hard
Simple words

Nothing more than another day like so many others
pushing carcasses
Or
Stripped bare
Doing what I'm paid to do

I see the smoke from the factory before I've even left the main road
It mixes with the smoke from the dried pet food factory that's just next door
Every day I ask myself
What's it like working at the pet food factory
What do they have to do
One of these weeks I'd like to see for myself

The smell of the abattoir from the moment I open the car door
Smell of meat of death of industry at five in the morning
Almost makes me feel like a mixed grill with fries and a quarter-litre carafe of red

The walkway into the factory is interminable
I have my ritual of giving my wedding band
A couple of kisses six times
Take a piss in the locker room
Put my earplugs in first then beard mask and put on my work coat
Left boot before the right
Always
No doubt a memory from an old ad for mineral water featuring Zidane

And even if I'll never be world champion of the factory
I make my way down into the arena
See the carcasses to be shifted like so many
Opponents
Limber up
Still feeling the effect of the anti-inflammatory taken with my full working breakfast
And it's onto the offensive
To work

The factory is
Above all else
A relationship with time
Time that passes

That doesn't pass
Trying not to look at the clock too much
No different to previous days

The boss comes by and greets me
I push my carcasses
Sometimes one catches me by surprise in the back
Shoved by another bloke
A thud
Muffled grunt
It's the goddamned back that cops
The axis of pain
Cervical spinal lumbar
A back in tatters

My arms are alright
You'd say they're looking built
My hands too

My mother said when she dropped by not long ago that before
I used to have an intellectual's hands
Before
That now my fingers had thickened
I remember that bloody stupid joke
'What's the difference between a worker and an intellectual'
'The worker washes his hands before taking a piss
The intellectual washes his afterwards'
I don't wash my hands anymore
Don't feel like turning into a schizo

We greet each other with a shake of the hand at clock-on
Same as anywhere else
Here
The handshakes are particularly firm
My hands don't get crushed anymore in those grips
But my back fuck
My spine screams at times
I speak coaxingly to my pain
'O still my suffering and try to hold your peace'

I push carcasses
It never ends
I'm only
Earning a living
No
Earning a few bucks
No
Selling my labour
That's right
That's how it is

When's the break
I sing to pass the time
Is this then how men live
Is this then how I'm living
And yet even when it doesn't make sense anymore
At the point when I can't go on
I work
And I tell all those dicks in social work
My so-called real profession
The ones who blew me off after every job interview

I tell them all to fuck off
I'm a worker that's what I am
I don't spend my time drinking coffee smoking ciggies
pontificating about inextricable situations
But no disdain here
No
No blowing up
Take a break
Have a coffee
Smoke some ciggies
That endless walkway
My wife on the telephone usually just woken up
Her soft voice before she's had her coffee
Then left boot first in the locker room again

I go back in
I'm pushing my bullocks
Sweating like a pig
Especially as the anti-inflammatories start to wear off
Another two hours and we can call it quits
Knock off
Another hour and a half
As long as a football match
And we'll see about tomorrow
Just an hour
It's getting sweeter
I'm no longer pushing with my arms my body my back
It uses my everything my nothing
Yes to pass the time I sing
It's over

Before leaving
I'm going to buy some cheap meat from the abattoir
supermarket
Meat that'll knock you out it's so good
That'll make you wanna kiss the Holy Virgin's arse
A skirt a rib-eye a hanger a flank and I don't know what
else that I'm going to eat back home with some potatoes
It's as if I had to feed myself from this meat
I push every day
As if it had to lend me some of its strength
May it lend me
Its strength

Back home
The dog licks my hands no doubt still impregnated
with the blood of the animals
There are leftovers from last night
An extraordinary sight
Your birthday
My love my wife my light
The roses sublime
As many as there are candles
The cadaver of a bottle of wine
Everything that is not the abattoir
Where tomorrow I must return
For another ordinary day

38.

Antoine Le Gurun died fighting for France
17 April 1917
Killed in action outside the Hurtebise Farm
At Chemin des Dames
That's what the minister's words say on the plaque

On this April 16 day in 2017
I'm on the island of Houat with my wife
Whose great-grandfather died on these battlefields
of mine
The war memorial
Features a soldier from the 33rd Colonial Infantry
Division
Locals from Houat had joined with the colonials
who were landing at nearby ports
Among the first to go over the top

Those days of the Nivelle Offensive
Days of snow on the plateau at Craonne
Days of sunshine on this little Breton island
One hundred years later
A stone's throw from the square of the town hall where
we were married
From the church where we were not joined in wedlock
And from the memorial where Antoine is the only
casualty from 1917 to feature

The café is closed
It's Easter Sunday
We're there in the evening
I had bought beers just in case to drink and to write
in his honour
In homage to him
Antoine Le Gurun
Fisherman
Died in the Great Slaughter
In the greatest most pointless offensive of the Great
Slaughter
But
Died for France

The Chemin des Dames
I went there a number of times
A pilgrimage almost
Even before knowing about Antoine
My local Champagne heritage and the memory
of invasions
Of battles
Of the war
Of wars
Of the stories my grandmother used to tell me

When we were married
In that town hall
In the square of this small Breton island
There was the memorial to the fallen
Friends were playing *The Internationale* in our honour
On the clarinet and the accordion

Hardly a thought was spared for Antoine but I'd like to think it gave him a laugh

About Antoine
There's not much to remember him by
Here
Except that he was a fisherman
Like all the others
Died in the war
Like so many others

Hurtebise Farm
The last time
I went there
By way of pilgrimage almost
With my wife
You see it's here
Where I belong
Not fishing grounds but battle grounds
Fields of death
Which amounts to the same thing
There are the living the dead and there's the water
There are the living the dead and there's the slaughter

What has this to do with the abattoir if not for the blood spilt in The Great Butchery

Perhaps just a few words from *The Song of Craonne*
The song I so often hum as I work

‘The ones with the dough
They’re the ones who’ll be back
It’s for them that the rest of us are taking the flack’

39.

Pok Pok
Dear pup

If you knew what it takes every day
When I come home to take you out for a walk

I'm on the edge of exhaustion
No not even on the edge
Utterly exhausted
Undone by fatigue
Ready to fall asleep on the spot as soon as I'm home

But every time I get home
The joy no something even more than joy of knowing
you're there behind the door
Alive
Wagging your tail your whole backside
In celebration of the fact that I'm back

You must love the smell of abattoir I exude
My hands that you lick like lollies
My clothes that you snuffle

Scarcely time to sit down
To unwind and de-stress
To have a beer
I've got to go out for a walk

Even if I just can't anymore
Even if sometimes I'm literally crying with tiredness

But it's hardly your fault
Young six-month-old pup
Amid all this business of human slaughter
You just want to run
To play
To cling fast to the ocean at our usual beach
Round up the birds
Dig in the sand again and again
Bring back pieces of wood and seaweed and run and play some more

You are alive my little Pok Pok
And here I am
Ruined by exhaustion
But so happy to see you alive and happy
It takes me away from the dead animals I've been working on all day long

I don't talk to you much about my days
I prefer to tell you that I'm weary but so happy to be working
To come back to find you at home
And to come now
We're going for a walk
Here we are at the beach
That I'm working so I'm able to pay for your dog biscuits
That's how it goes with us humans

What would you make of it if I were to tell you exactly
what goes on at the abattoir
Would you look at me differently
Would you see me as an agent of the banality of evil
An ordinary son of a bitch
The guy who is playing his part just a link in the chain
of the whole foul business and absolves himself for any
number of perfectly valid reasons

It is perhaps appalling to say but were the bosses to ask
me to slaughter the beasts
I'd do it
You have to work
When I'm on break I sometimes overhear the guys
doing the slaughtering
Shake their hand
Chat a bit
They look no worse nor better than me
Have a look in their eyes just as distant just as weary
Not the look of bloodthirsty barbarians
Perhaps
Doubtless
Some of them too have a dog they love
I don't know

The factory is wreaking havoc with my body
My convictions
All I thought I knew of work and rest
Of weariness
Of joy
Of humanity

How can one feel so happy from this weariness
This inhumane job
I still don't know
I used to think I only went there
To be able to pay for your biscuits
And the vet from time to time
Not for this weariness nor this joy

Come on Pok Pok
Just a few more minutes of walking
I'm tired
I can't anymore

Tomorrow
I have to go to work
And when I get home
Tomorrow
We'll go for a longer walk I hope
But right now I'm done

Tomorrow I'll feel better
Just have to rest between now and then
Get a good sleep
Tomorrow little Pok Pok I swear
If you knew
Tomorrow

40.

Once loaded
The trucks at the docks will depart for Rungis
Italy Guingamp Greece
Or somewhere else

I had however been warned
'You'll see
The loading
It's physical'
Shrug of the shoulders
It's pushing carcasses
Here or somewhere else

There are five of us on loading
Plus one supervisor
As for how physical the work is
You have to connect the rails from the factory to the trucks
The switch plates are crappy
Poorly designed
The hooks from which the animals hang often need to be changed
The trucks aren't level
Meaning that often
The rails slant upwards

And you have to push
The carcasses along rails angled up like the crosses of
Golgotha

One truck
It's a good hour of labour at least
The pace is frightening
Screaming and shouting in all directions to make sure
your workmate has heard the order
Three times each time
Despite the racket of the factory
'Load load load
Push push push'
Sometimes you forget a switch plate
'Rail rail rail
Fucking hell
Rail rail rail'
Too late
A pig carcass or a cow has fallen
Five of us are onto it
Get the beast back onto the hook
We're sweating and silent

Two hundred and fifty pigs a truck
Each of us loading three animals at a time
That's six hooks each bearing half a pig
Set the switch plate
And you have to push
You really have to cram them into that truck
Whether it's bullocks or pigs
You're sweating again just trying to find a sliver of space

Pushing away like the damned
Where will you find a spot to shove these last animals in
The trucks are spewing them back out
We're pretty much spewing too

At five
Only white guy in a team of blacks
I try to act like I'm the guy on the basketball team who's
there for his height and his ability to lift off the hooks
without needing the metal stool which can be used
somewhere else
Three trucks to be done at once
We divide ourselves up as best we can
We'll regroup in an hour
At best

Sometimes we wait for a truck
Ten minutes of suspended time perhaps even fifteen
We've finished readying the rails and the animals
By some extraordinary privilege
Implicit and tolerated
We're outside
We've pushed open the emergency exit door
We're half-hiding behind a large pillar so we can't be
seen by the big bosses in their offices whose windows
look out over us
We're out in the fresh air of spring which has arrived
Feeling the sun and the warmth and smelling the trees
blossoming in the industrial zone
There's the smell of our bodies too
All huddled in where we are behind our pillar

But we're outside
Ten good minutes
We dream of lighting up a cigarette but
We don't dare
The truck's coming
The madness returns

Until now
I'd eat nothing at break but a sandwich
Just a snack
But as of day two
Now I've worked out
You need a meal
A proper one
That will keep you going until the end of the afternoon
Later even
If the trucks are held up
At the abattoir's canteen
There's dish of the day lasagna beef burgundy sirloin
How's the veal stew
The stew's good
Make it ourselves
Goes well with the rice and fills you up good and proper

Getting back to it is hard on your digestion and there are trucks still to be loaded
Knock-off time is calculated not in hours
But in trucks
How many trucks still to go
Will they be on time
Are the rails at the right height

Fucking truck come on
I'm sick of waiting for you
Sitting outside in the sun
I'd rather be in the cold
Loading you up
So we can be done with it.

It's late
The truck's not coming
We're waiting
We're mucking around shouting
'Truck truck truck'
Trying to make it come

Our energy has been devoured
The midday meal is long gone
We're hoping for a glimpse of a distant moving shadow
reflected in the office windows of the bosses
Who are long gone too
We're no longer hiding but still we don't dare smoke
We're only waiting for one thing
Just one more truck
Just one more hour

41.

‘I have nothing to say of this underworld place. I know it happened and that I and the texts I write shall henceforth bear its mark.’

Georges Perec
Places of Deceit

My life would never have been the same without psychoanalysis
My life will never again be the same after the factory

The factory is a couch

42.

A student of history
He's been at the abattoir since his end-of-term exams finished up
He's in the last year of his degree I think
But I'm afraid I don't know exactly what it is he's working on seeing as he never goes out for a smoke and he's on the line two places down from me

Every day
He's running late
Oh it's never by much
Five minutes in the morning
Two minutes getting back after the break
Enough to be irritating

From what I've been told he keeps screwing things up too
Usually just careless
But happens often
Too often
Doesn't matter that he's told repeatedly by a workmate that he has to
Push six carcasses along rail number twenty-three then three along rail twelve
He'll push
And mix up the number of the rail and carcasses or vice versa

A good hour and a half late this morning
He blows in happy as Larry
Cops a first shot across the bow from the looks we fire at him
A second from the boss
I catch snatches of conversation and it touches a nerve

A workmate says to me
'Oh you know he's working in a different timeframe to us
For him it's history
He's taking the long-term view
For us it's the factory'

The long term
And suddenly there he is
Good old Fernand Braudel
Historian
Hitting me right in the gob
Smack bang in the middle of the abattoir
Goddamn it Fernand
If only you knew
That an uneducated labourer was invoking you without even knowing
It makes me laugh and dream
Of you my dear old Fernand and your Mediterranean in the age of Philip II

And if
Like you Fernand
We had to act on the basis that neither the factory nor Philip were the objects of our studies anymore

But merely the setting
I'd still have to find my Mediterranean

That said
We soon hear the reason for the tardiness

It's hot very hot a Brittany heatwave
Batteries in the alarm clock couldn't cope

And we all have a laugh like we do every morning
when there's an excuse

A student of stories

43.

Turns out my last day came quicker than expected
Decided the night before to be precise

Considering
That I'm going to find a few weeks' work again
Supervising my handicapped guys
That I'd already told everyone at the abattoir
That I hadn't really thought too hard about it and
That I'd get more or less the same amount in
unemployment benefits for a month as I would from
the factory working three weeks
That enough was enough after five months straight
without a break

Would just as soon not be bored shitless wrecking my
back my arms and everything else
And take some leave

So that's it
No notice
No worries
Only a few more hours pushing carcasses
And then it's goodbye

The moment arrives
I'm done
Some guys come and see me to wish me good luck down
the track

The news didn't take long to do the rounds of the carcasses

I do a round of the factory to take my leave and thank all those with whom I've had the pleasure of going through hell for five months

We have a bit of a vent
Some stop to take five minutes away from their station
An eternity

Outside we have one last coffee as we have a few smokes
We talk about my new job about the factory about our families and about life

It's my mate Morgan who has the last word
'Right then
Seeing as you never know what's round the corner we're super happy for you and really hope you find a proper job in your field
And if you don't and you come back
We'll also be super happy'
Me too
I think
In fact I'm sure of it

And may the time that causes everything to fade not cause me too quickly to forget your faces and your names
Your voices and the dignity of your labour
My comrades
My heroes

44.

I had to go back
Still no work except for at the factory
And no sooner am I back
Than I'm celebrating my birthday at the abattoir

My workmates have a tradition of bringing in packets of Lutti brand Harlequin lollies to 'mark an occasion'

Marking an occasion might mean announcing some good news
Going on holidays
Starting a job somewhere other than the factory
A birthday

So at break time I hand out a lolly to everyone
'You can't be about to leave again when you've only been back a week
So it must mean it's your birthday'
Everybody's sucking their lollies
Eyes wide with childlike joy

Two stories do the rounds as to why it's this particular lolly
The first would have it that the big big boss
The one whose name is uttered with as much respect as fear
Always keeps a basket of Harlequin lollies in his office
and that you can help yourself whenever you're called in

At least
That's the story
And reappropriation by the workers subverts this symbol of their employers

The other would have it that the most skilful suckers
Keep their lolly in their mouth for an hour
And eight lollies a day means
The working day is done
And that time goes faster sucking a lolly the way
Beckett's characters suck stones

Been back at the abattoir a week
Nothing has changed while I was on my
Month and a half road trip
Here
It's still the same trip still the same tripe

Still on autopilot
The same carcasses
The same offal

I went back
No more difficult than getting back into it after the summer
No other joy than that of catching up with workmates

They weren't expecting to see me again
Gave me a big welcome between two carcasses
The day after my return
A workmate

Don’t know who
Secretly slipped a lolly into my pocket

45.

Fucking strike
We'll be doing overtime for the rest of the week trying to catch up the time lost today
Hardly a permanent on the job this morning
The usual casuals obviously
And not a single red supervisor's hard hat missing at roll call

Inevitably things go slower
Guys who don't know how to work the machines
Work the right levers
Switch the right rails

The carcasses must be having a good old laugh
Relishing their vengeance
Posthumously
Vying with each other to crash down
About fifteen of them over the course of the day
Welcome to hell

The official text of the labour laws provides however pursuant to Article L.1242-6: 'It is prohibited to enter into a fixed-term employment contract for the purpose of replacing an employee whose employment contract is suspended due to a collective labour dispute'
Yet you see casuals and jobbers clocked on for the day
Regardless of what the law provides

The old hands at the abattoir also tell how in the good old days the casuals would picket outside the factory with the permanent employees
Burning pallets
Barbecues with choice pieces of meat emerging from everywhere
Never-ending slabs of beer

Alas
Today it's clear the way things stand
For a casual who strikes
Which he's nonetheless entitled to do
It's goodbye and farewell
A clear display of employers' logic

They ask me to start early
There's a barrowful of us no-hopers in precarious employment
One good thing I'm at my usual station

I dream of going on strike
Like when I used to have a real job and I was risking nothing
I dream of being able to go to the demo
But I know that by the time I get home I'll be too knackered
I dream of my permanent mates all good and warm in their beds and who'll doubtless shortly be earning respect as they make their way along in the protest with all their 'CGT Abattoir' union flags
A fit gang of strikers strong of arm and gaze

I would have fitted in well applying a bit of pressure
to the cops outside the council buildings
I would have been so happy to be one of those
'illiterates' who Macron shits all over
One of those who aren't working so they can afford a
suit but a polar fleece from the Decathlon store given
how cold it is at work
To be part of that collective force and to joke about the
slackers he presumes we are
Eh Manu
Aren't you going to come and have a laugh with us while
we push a few carcasses tomorrow morning

The march was leaving at ten-thirty from the factory
parking lot so they could join up with the general
protest
I look at the clock when it gets to that hour and time
seems so slow
The outdoors so far away
Six and a half hours I've been slogging away at the tails
and racks I have to hang
At one point I burst out laughing
I imagine a black bloc from the abattoir that hijacks all
the gear from the factory
Saws knives hooks forklifts high-pressure hoses *e tutti
quanti*
A mighty handy group of protest leaders that would
make
That's no student demo
A supervisor hears my laugh and asks me if I'm alright

‘Yes it’s nothing a nervous laugh you know not many
guys on today and nothing’s working
Might as well laugh’
‘Right you are best way to take it’

Nothing’s working and that’s a euphemism
Now my new conveyor belt decides to go on strike too
The only three mechanics who know how it works are
striking too
Fucking strike

Just two more hours of dragging tops and I’ll be finished
dragging carrying pushing heaving using only the
strength in my arms
I pray to Saint Karl that I not be condemned on the altar
of the industrial revolution as the scab it might appear
that I am

My arms will have held out
And the strike I hope does too

Onwards Marx

46.

Sunday

Like every Sunday evening
I'm dragging the chain a bit more than usual
More than I should

I'm making the most of things for just a bit longer
Even if I know
That I'll pay for it even more dearly
When I get up and afterwards at clock-on

Sunday
Day of the Lord
Rest of the week
Days of gore

Monday

I can't find the time to write
Too much work
Too weary

At home
The daily grind
Housework to do

When I don't do it
It's my relationship that suffers

Tuesday

Goddamned aches and pains when I get up and dress
The weekend is still distant
Today is Tuesday so tomorrow is Wednesday and that'll
mean having survived half the week

An eternal round of cows to be broken down

Dairy cows
Holstein

Multipurpose breeds
Montbéliarde
Normande

Beef cattle
Charolaise
Rouge des prés
Limousin
Blonde d'Aquitaine

We finish in time

Wednesday

Monotony
Grinding
Sweet
Or sordid

Nothing changes

Same mugs at the same time
Same ritual before clocking on
Same physical pain
Same automaton movements
Same cows parading past now and always to be broken down on this line that never stops
That will never stop
Same factory surrounds
Same conveyor belt
Same workmates locked into position
And the cows parade past
Same movements

Sometimes it's as reassuring as a cocoon
You do it without even realising
Thoughts wandering
The only true freedom is within
Factory you shall never have my soul
I am here
And I count for so much more than you
And I count so much more because of you
Thanks to you
Here I am on the shores of childhood
My world not yet darkened by death
I'm at my grandmother's
A warm eternal presence
She'll still be there tomorrow
I smile as I break down my cows

Some small sadness surfaces in the memories and now
the carcass becomes the enemy
My actions though automatic require effort then trigger
pain
Everything is so heavy
The cows
My body
The work
My life no less
It all weighs so heavily in this place that doesn't change
Will never change
My grandmother has been dead for ages
I'll soon be forty and here I am rotting away working
in an abattoir

Most often
It's nothing like those two extremes
There's nothing but the robotic monotony of cows to be
broken down
And the counting and calculations
Counting the hours still to get through
The minutes to the next hour
The number of cows I can push in a single shove
The number of hooks I can grab in a single hand
The hours I've already worked in the week
The rails of cows still to be taken away
You calculate your effort
Count your limbs check they're all there
And your aches and pains
I count and re-count
Because

It's just as Brel says in the song
'With these people
You don't talk
You don't talk
You count'

It's Wednesday and it's the middle of the week
I don't know if it's the monotony or the repetitive
straining that's so exhausting whereas yesterday and on
Monday I was doing alright goddamn it
And still two more days to get through
And tomorrow yet another fucking day of strikes
It'll be awful again
Clock on at four in the morning to make up for the
delays
Wake up two hours earlier to have time for coffee for a
walk with the dog to roll your smokes ahead of time
to get on the road have a coffee in the smokers' shelter to
have time for the rituals and the grinding monotony

Thursday

As expected
The alarm bites and it's hard hard hard
Like last week there's a team of jobbers to replace
the usual permanents
Strangely last week's strikers arrive at the usual clock-on
time
The jobbers vanish
Work is sluggish
As if they were half on strike half on the job

They won't be back after the break
I hear from a non-striking workmate that they've done
their four hours of work which equates to the number
of hours overtime allowed per week so they won't be
out of pocket which I consider particularly astute
The jobbers return

Time drags
Drags on and fucking on
Stretches out to infinity

A red hard hat goes past and asks if I can work Saturday
You can never be required to work Saturday mornings
but you get paid three hours overtime even if you only
work one
I answer yes
And the two remaining hours seem even longer looking
at a weekend that's dead in the water

The end of the day turns to shit
I thought I'd be finished with work tomorrow knowing
that today was going to be the toughest day
Like hell
'They say time is a bastard slipping away
That it makes a cloak of our sorrows'
I've got to the point where I'm humming Carla Bruni
when I'm dreaming of being on strike
A fine example of the aporia of the universe and its
sacred cows

Friday

We call on whatever remains of our strength so we can finish more quickly
And indeed we wind it all up a whole half-hour early
We use the time to wander around the factory and lend a hand to mates working in other sections so they can get ahead a little

Friday afternoon
Back home it should be party time
But it never is
I'm irritable
That's an understatement
Irascible

'Friday-itis' we say now my wife and I smiling
As if it's a sickness that has finally been diagnosed

As if
All the accumulated subconscious stress
The accumulated physical pain and exhaustion
The accumulated boredom of time that never passes
The accumulated days at the factory
Every day at the factory
Every one of them since I entered the machine over a year ago already and my departure which I really can't envisage
The fact of having to get back in the saddle on Monday for another week
The fact of having to rest on the weekend

As if
The perpetual paradigm that provides that if you don't
keep your head together your body will give out
And that if you don't keep your body together your
head will explode

As if everything was exploding at the end of every week

There you go
Back to the land of the living
But I still don't know how to cross the Styx that is
Friday without paying my obol of anger

Saturday

One fat hour of work
Three hours' pay
The week has finished well

Tomorrow is Sunday
Tomorrow there'll still be some enjoyment to be had
from the freedom of the living
Tomorrow there'll still be a reluctance to go to bed early
All the while certain that I'll pay for it dearly on Monday
when I get up and afterwards at work
There'll always be time for a new week
One more week

47.

'Sales reps are the scum of the earth
Should all be exterminated'
Philou had given me fair warning a few months earlier

The sales reps are the guys who spend their day at the factory tagging cows that I'm going to have to get down from their rails quick smart because there's been an order and the sales rep knows for a fact which beast will satisfy the customer's expectations
That's his job

The sales reps all wear red hard hats
Wear them proudly
Because they know

They know which cow's for which customer
And generally
Evidently
The cow that the customer thinks he wants that the sales rep knows he wants
Is right at the back of the rail
Always
And you have to stop everything else and get that one down

Meaning that I get to shift about twenty or so carcasses off the main rail

That I have to keep feeding the production line with the shit we were handling before the sales dude showed up
That I have to sort
And then sort again

One goddamned sales rep tag means half an hour of guaranteed fucking around

On top of it all it's not as though those dicks help with pushing a carcass or two
Oh no
I'm sweating away trying to manage the bends and they're gazing love-struck at the cows
And while everybody else tries to lend a hand
The sales reps no
They look at the animals
At best give them a pat
And have a whinge that
'It's not a great day for sales'

I've just brought the animal he tagged out from the back
Filled a holding rail
Just happy it's done
Dazed
And the sales rep
He adopts a thoughtful look
And wham
He tags another animal right at the back of the holding rail I've just filled

Doesn't matter how many times I say
'For fuck's sake aren't you done yet with your pain-in-the-arse bullshit'
Like I have every day for six months
He replies
'Yeah yeah'
And skips off to another rail

Today
I've been reduced to asking the boss for help sorting my cows
It's the first time in my career as a labourer that
I've had to make a blatant request for help from the boss
It's the last straw though
That arsehole of a sales rep just tagged three animals
at the back of three rails

It's Patrice who shows up about five minutes later
It's eleven o'clock and usually we'd be finishing up
in another two hours but with the shit the other guy dumped on me
I spot the rep's red hard hat slipping out of the fridge
on the down low
I go take a look
Another animal has been tagged
The last one on the rail

'Bitch'
I yell

Patrice hurries over laughing already
'Where'

I pull it together
'That guy in his red hard hat
He just left and he's tagged another animal the bastard'

We're laughing though as we push

48.

'Speak not of poetry
Speak not of poetry
As you crush the wild flowers
And let the light and clarity play
In the corners of a grey-walled yard
Where dawn at last might have its day'

Barbara
Perlimpinpin

We sing at the factory
Goddamn how we sing
We hum in our heads
We scream at the top of our lungs drowned out by the noise of the machines
We whistle the same persistent tune for two hours
We have the same stupid song in our heads that we heard on the radio that morning
There's no more beautiful way to pass the time
And it helps you cope
Thinking about something else
About forgotten lyrics
Helps put a smile on your face

When I don't know what to sing
I go back to the basics
The Internationale
Cherry Time

The Bloody Week
Trenet
It'll always be Trenet now and forever
The great Charles 'without whom we would all be
accountants' to quote Jacques Brel
Trenet who injects some joy into this god-awful abattoir
who makes me smile at my wife when *I Have Your Hand*
in my hand and then there's *The Mad Lament* still the
most beautiful song of all time or *Ménilmontant*
The Poets' Soul
Let me list them
Reggiani of course Daniel Darc Nougaro Brel Philip
Buty Fersen Fréhel and the Little Sparrow Vian Jonasz
les Frères Jacques or Bashung the Wampas Ferrat
Bourvil Stromae NTM Anne Sylvestre and there'll
always be Leprest and Barbara

But Trenet
Trenet takes me away from this work this factory life
Every day
Without him without his absolute genius
I know for sure I would not have held out
I would not be holding out
And it's true too that Barbara gave me hope once more
as I listened to her song *The Pain of Living* one evening
a long time ago now when everything was so black so
black enough to want to put an end to it all

You Charles you're like a towering Chaplin making
these hellish modern times somehow bearable

It's the genius of your bewitching refrains that pushes
my carcasses that helps me bear the pain and hold out
for the break and then for knock-off time
It's your *Devil's Java* when nothing's going right
It's *The Beach Piano* when I hope things will brighten
It's *The Phantom* I am every morning back on the job
It's *The Years of My Youth* before the factory
It's my *Mad Lament* that I just have to write

For many
Including me
There's the popular
Sanson Souchon Julien Clerc Joe Dassin Vanessa
Paradis Cloclo Sardou Pierre Bachelet Julien Doré
Michel Delpech Bruel Cabrel Goldman Calogero who
plays music and good old Pierrot Perret

For everybody
There are the drinking songs
The bawdy songs
And may Dudule's dick delight the priest from Camaret
while Fanchon whose godmother's still Breton keeps
looking for a little white wine from over Nogent way

Except for the days you go without
The other day during my break I overheard a workmate
say to one of her colleagues
'D'you know it's been so full on today I haven't even had
time to sing'
I think it's one of the most beautiful the most true and
the most awful sentences I've ever heard uttered about

the condition of the working class
Those moments when it is so unspeakable you don't
even have time to sing
You just watch the belt relentlessly advance your
anxiety rising in the face of the inevitability of the
machine and you're forced to keep processing no matter
what with
No time even to sing
And hell knows there are days you don't

Let me come back to Barbara
'I'm no poet
I'm a woman who sings'
So she liked to say

No poetry at the factory either
At best we're just people who sing as we work
The smoke from the factory at Clohars-Carnoët is the
same as the smoke in Lorient in Priziac or in Chicago or
the fire of Billancourt
Inside
That's us

What poetry is there to be had from the machine the
driving rhythm and the brutish repetition
From the machines that never work or that run too
quickly
In that endless neon night of wanly illuminated white-
tiled walls and stainless-steel tables and conveyor belts
and god-awful brown floors

From the dead animals we work on all night long and
into the morning
No bird ever finds its way through a hidden opening
into our workrooms
The only living animals are the rats we battle near the
bins outside
We never see any living cows
Our faces are at best like portraits by Otto Dix
Our bodies atlases of musculoskeletal issues
Our delights small nothings
Scraps of insignificance that take on meaning and
beauty in the grand totality the great nothingness of
the factory
A mate who can tell you need a hand just by the look in
your face
An action that becomes efficient
A machine that breaks down for ten minutes and the
muscles that relax
The weekend that will be here soon
The day that eventually ends
The looking forward to a drink before dinner
Eating your fill
Sleeping to your heart's content
Your pay that finally comes through
Having done a good day's work
Having recalled a song you'd forgotten that'll see you
through another two hours
Remembered a verse
Smiling

'Speak no longer of poetry
Speak no longer of poetry
But let the wild flowers grow
And the light and clarity play
In the corners of a grey-walled yard
Where dawn at last might have its day'

And finish with what could be an autumn or spring time haiku

No more poetry
Wild flowers and nothing more
Light and clarity

Of spring time

49.

The butchers didn't look particularly upbeat
Yesterday when they visited the abattoir
They looked serious
Considered
Focused

They wandered about in groups of ten between the
carcasses led by a red hard hat
I couldn't help but see it as some strange tango

Everything had been cleaned for their arrival
Polished
Buffed
As if
There were no need for any bloodletting

It's the factory's corporate image
Obviously
One hundred and eighty butchers from all over Brittany
representing so many potential customers
And they're being pampered

At the entrance to my fridge they've hung a prize
specimen whose weight the butchers are supposed to
guess at the end of the day on a card given to them when
their visit is over
'Be sure to write the weight down to the first decimal
of the number of grams'

The prize animal whose weight the butchers have to
guess has been gussied up with ribbons and rosettes in
red white and blue
It's as handsome as an agricultural show from yesteryear

A rail stretches out behind the prize beast with our
finest carcasses as if to mask our everyday work

The butchers arrive in clusters

From my fridge at a distance all I can see is their feet

They have blue plastic shoe covers
Fuss over the animal whose weight they're supposed to
guess
Head off again

I see a butcher stick his head behind the stage curtain of
this theatre to look at the rest of the fridge
Our eyes meet
I give him a smile brother to brother and sincerely hope
he wins just for his curiosity and that scrap of humanity
That small pleasure

Apart from that
The day was as flat monotonous and difficult as
every day at the factory

Today
You could donate blood at the abattoir's multipurpose
room

Just the idea made me laugh
Although there was the fact that it had been ages since
I had done it

That morning I had decided I was going to
Was determined

And then
The collection times coincide with those of my shift

And then
I grow increasingly weary as the day goes by

And then
I don't dare ask the boss to get somebody to replace me
for an hour so I can donate blood because everyone
already has a shitload to do

And then
Well goddamn it
Fucking supervisors
If you want people to donate blood
Go donate your own

And then I'm not about to cut short my lunch break and
then if I go and I feel faint when I go back in and then
I want to go home and then and then and then there are
just so many reasons to abandon the whole idea

And
As if by miracle

We finish the job early
The boss wants to wrangle me to go off to lend a hand
loading a truck full of pigs heading to Rungis
I ask him if I can't go and donate blood instead

When it's my turn
The doc asks me if I've suffered any 'significant
accidental exposure to blood during the previous year'
Excuse me
He had misread his questionnaire
He had forgotten the adjective 'human' before the word
'blood'

Apart from that
Tomorrow I'm heading back to the factory
To get my daily dose of blood

The butchers weren't upbeat
The same could be said of me

50.

In the mornings it's night
In the afternoons it's night
The night is even worse

From the moment you're back in the factory it's night
The neon lights
The absence of windows in all of our giant cube-shaped work rooms
A night that will last as long as our eight-hour-minimum shift

You emerge from sleep still stained by dreams of the factory
Only to dive back into another night
Artificial cold and neon-lit

From that point on
It's as if
It were an extension of your night

Between the night of home and that of the job
Waking
Two hours of transition
Bleary eyes and double espressos
That'd be morning then
All the world's mornings

In the locker room before the shift starts
Another five minutes before diving back into the night
I genuinely admire all the men and women working here
who are showered and perfumed
I just can't do it
Showering is an evening thing
At least
Something you do when you get home from work

Some people really doll themselves up
Must really spend some time in front of the mirror

The factory mirrors
There are some at the intersections and at the right-
angled corners of the endless corridors so you can see
the forklift trucks coming and can avoid being run over
You don't use them to look at yourself
Anyway you know what you look like
White blood-stained uniform same as everybody else
Weary bodies
Eyes that are still open

Not me
The factory is a uniform I wear for a week and that gets
increasingly filthy and rank as the days go by

Into the machine on Friday or Saturday

I imagine for those others
It must be a question of dignity or some noble
sentiment

To arrive at the abattoir clean and smelling good
Despite what they're going to have to do

In the morning
Between my two nights
I'm here without being here
As if
I was in some liminal state
Real life will resume at knock-off time

I want to believe that when I'm at the factory
I'm in some liminal space
Waiting to find something better
Even if it's been a year and a half already and I still
haven't found it
I want to believe
That I'm here without being here

So
In this world of nights
There's no morning no evening nor even any night
There are only neon lights illuminating the shop floor
where the blood-stained uniforms work
Some people have showered beforehand
Others not

Mostly there are
All those mornings in the world
When everybody in his night
Dreams

Of a world with no factories
Of a morning with no nights

51.

I have the factory to thank for the fact I no longer suffer panic attacks

Or rather I don't

I can date the time I stopped suffering bloody panic attacks to when I started at the factory
Terrible
Irremediable
Infinity and its void crashing down on your head
Bringing out a cold sweat vertigo madness and death

I can date the time I stopped having to take medication to when I started at the factory
Psychotropics
Anxiolytics
Stabilisers
Antidepressants

For a long time I was scared of going mad
A very long time

That was my main anxiety
The mother of them all
The one that would trigger an attack and attacks like so many symptoms
So much suffering that was as regular in its daily manifestation as it was intolerable

Perhaps the ordeal that is the factory has substituted
itself for the ordeal of that anxiety
That would be the most logical link
Having to endure day after day night after night hour
after hour
A simple transfer of symptoms
It's no longer the mind that is suffering but the body
And that is quite enough suffering

In particular
Well after I'd stopped the Lacanian psychoanalysis
The factory spat back the hours and hours I'd spent on
the couch right back in my face

The parallels are obvious
Or so it seems to me
What am I here for
What's the point
Why am I having these thoughts at precisely this
moment
Why talk why be silent why write
For what
The role of psychoanalysis is to have you stretched out
on a couch and talking
The role of the factory is to have you on your feet
having to work and be silent
And paradoxically
Given the time you have to think at the factory when
your body is working
My anxieties ought to have manifested even more
acutely

This is not my place my job my life what the fuck am I doing here after all my years of study after everything I've read written or understood about the meaning of the world

But no

Quite the contrary

The factory has calmed me down like a couch

If I'd had to go mad
It would have been in those first days on the prawns on the crumbed fish or at the abattoir
It would have been the night of the tofu

Finishing at the factory will be like finishing therapy
It will be simple and crystal-clear like a truth
My truth

I have to put up with this ordeal for as long as there is work still to be done
Or this work for as long as the ordeal persists

This ordeal

This work

They will be

And by writing these words just as you would speak into
the benevolent ear and mind of a therapist
I realise that no

I owe the factory no more than I owe to therapy

I have love to thank
I have my strength to thank
I have my life to thank

52.

The horse drops struck down just like the cows the calves the lambs

The animals' blood spurts runs floods out in great gushes

The Blood of the Beasts is a documentary made by Georges Franju in 1949 in the abattoirs of Vaugirard and La Villette that makes any video produced by L.214 look like a cute episode of *Little House on the Prairie*

The Blood of the Beasts is unbearable and that is why it should be seen
Because it's a precise depiction of the job
Because it's not a covert video shot by militant 'animal activists'
Because seventy years later
In essence nothing has changed
Except for the personal protective equipment
The saws which are now electric
Even if every factory shop floor still has a good old handsaw in the event of the machinery breaking down
And the fact you can't smoke on the job anymore

The feeling of seeing your workmates
And all those animals passing in a never-ending parade
Their fat and their blood from which I shall forever be inured
Their death too

And those on the inside
As I am on the inside
Singing Trenet
'With the simple good humour of killers whistling or singing as they slit the throats'

53.

'Total number of animals'
It's written on a sheet printed in triplicate next to the
computer where the weight of the carcasses is recorded
Where the team gathers around before the shift starts to
see what the day holds

Less than five hundred animals and there are smiles
all round high fives it's going to be a good day
Between five hundred and five hundred and fifty animals
and it's all good it's not as bad as if it were worse
Between five hundred and fifty and six hundred and
you'll usually finish just in time if all goes well
More than six hundred and faces scowl and it already
feels like shit with overtime and bloody hell the day's
telling you it's going to be long
More than seven hundred animals is not something
I've seen yet but it appears it's around the corner with
the holiday season and that'll be a proper carnage
Worse than a butcher's shop

I go over to the computer that records the weight
Like I do every morning

'Total number of animals'
Six hundred and sixty-six

My mate Nico a metalhead who makes a pilgrimage to
Hellfest whenever Satan plays still hasn't seen the sheet

and asks me how many
I tell him
He bursts out laughing
Puts his hand in the air
Index finger and pinkie extended

I reckon only he could take that as a good omen

54.

'It's the most bloody annoying thing trying to find a
fingertip on the floor'
Jean-Paul's busy telling me
'With the blood and all the meat scraps that are
constantly lying around
A fingertip for god's sake
You can easily miss it
But he was strong Brendan was
He didn't even pass out
Cock-up with the automatic lift-arm
Got his finger jammed
Cut off at the first knuckle'

A kid of twenty-two who works here like so many others
waiting for something better
Namely an electrician's apprenticeship that the
government agency's refusing to pay for

A chopped-off finger
The graft didn't take
That's today's news

Today I almost buggered my finger on a meat hook
My femur on a chute
Made me stop and think about my workmate Brendan
Freshly amputated at the age of twenty-two

As a result of failing to touch wood

I'm touching bone

Those of my own carcass
Those of the cows

55.

Mum

I know you're worried about me just as you've worried about me your whole life

I know it turns your stomach and is affecting your health

I know my work at the factory worries you even if you say nothing to me about not finding a 'real' job of being forty soon and having spent so long studying all that and for what

I know you've worked hard all your life especially to pay for my schooling that you've made such huge sacrifices to give me a good education which I think I have had
Maybe you think it's a waste to end up at the factory
Frankly I probably agree
What you can't know is that it's because of those very studies that I'm coping and that I am able to write

Know that for this I am so profoundly grateful

As for the rest of it yes there have been periods that have been tougher than others yes you bravely carry on and sometimes you take a tumble but we have always picked ourselves up

This is only a stage
It is what it is
To be faced with courage and determination

And I would rather you know what my day involves than be stuck imagining the worst

It might for example involve going to the calf offal section an hour after clocking on

When my belly is still warm and full of a hearty breakfast
It might involve retrieving the heads and pluck respectively
The calves' mouths are ajar
Tongues dangling out from half-open jaws
The tag with the slaughter number corresponding to the offal of the animal to be retrieved is slipped between the tongue and palate
You have to give it a good tug to see if it's the right number
Or else put the tag back where it belongs

The calves can't look at me anymore with their cold dead eyes
Some of them still have the cartridge from the matador who stunned them before they were bled
A little blue disc at their forehead that slammed into their brain and made them lose consciousness

And as for the pluck
A collective noun for the heart spleen sweetbread liver and lungs
It's slippery and hard to pick up

When I get back to the work room
I pack up the head and pluck separately into two big bags
Hang them on hooks that each bear half a calf

Or I might be sent to the cow offal section
One heart two kidneys two cheeks one tongue one liver and sometimes a paunch if the customer asks for it
The paunch means the tripe
In a small work room near the udders horns and skins
The tripe hangs and drips like one of my memories from Naples
Minus the sun and the heat
In the white monotony of the factory

In order to bag up the cow offal
You have to separate them
Liver into one bag
Each time I think of you and how you love liver and of me and how I hate it and I block my nose as I lift up those slippery stinking livers each one weighing five kilos telling myself they would make some delicious steaks for you
Other offal into another bag
I have my own ritual of bagging up the heart first
Tongues kidneys and cheeks
The order doesn't matter so much

'Because the heart
Is life'
I repeat to myself every time like a fool

It's an ordinary Wednesday I don't know how I'm
managing
Not to hold the pen
It has been quite some time since I wrote with a pen
But pressing the keys of the computer which
Combine to
Form words then sentences
In time with my exhausted waning thoughts

Means ignoring it all even the factory and the fact
you could
Truly
Weep
From exhaustion
It has happened to me a few times
Alas not just from time to time
Returning home from work
Sitting down on the couch for five minutes
And then
Like
A great huge enormous blackhead you haven't seen that
bursts the minute you touch it
I think back on my day
Feel my muscles relax
And
Burst into the tears I've held back
Trying to be proud and dignified

And it will pass
As everything does
The fatigue the pain and the tears
Today I have not wept

It means remembering our weekly Sunday phone call
one or two months ago
When you must have heard my weary voice and asked
me had I worked the previous day
'Yes'
'And how much do you earn if you work on a Saturday'
'Oh, probably around fifty euros'

We had spoken of other things
That week
I received a letter from you
With a cheque for fifty euros
And a sweet note telling me to make the most
Of my weekend
Of my days off
Of my wife

My eyes welled up with tears at your maternal love at
such discreet thoughtfulness
Not so much for the money as for the unassuming
kindness of the gesture

So you see
Everything is alright
Dry your tears if you have any

Everything is alright
I have work
I'm working hard
But it's nothing
We're still standing

Your son who loves you

56.

'Pre-chilling is the process of progressive cooling of carcasses in a ventilated area of plus two degrees Celsius for the purposes of obtaining a core temperature of plus seven degrees Celsius within twenty-four hours' as I'm instructed by a website specialising in butchery

Said pre-chilling fridge is the first station situated on the mezzanine just below the slaughter hall
The half-carcasses come down on a toboggan-like rail
They follow a network of rails in an 'S' formation and progress on their own by means of what are known as 'drivers' while the air or water or I don't know what else is sprayed by a machine to bring down the temperature of the carcasses

Then comes that part of the chilling process requiring physical labour
This involves pushing and shunting the carcasses into the cold store before they are then quartered the next day
It's a bit like playing Tetris you push you add you remove you put back depending on the rails that are still free or that become available in the cooler
But there's no rail that disappears as if by magic here
It's a matter of plugging the holes as best you can

Same type of animals with the same type of animals
No question of hanging a steer next to a cull cow that's

going to end up as dry pet food after de-boning and
even less so next to a prize animal that's going to sell
at ten euros a kilo per half-carcass

In short you have to do as many batches as there are
available rails
All par for the course for any carcass dispatcher
Sure
But at the pre-chilling stage
There's the progress of the 'driver'
Those little pegs that make the animals advance along
their rails
The progress of the chain
Inexorable
At the relentless rhythm of one animal per minute
Sixty an hour

And
Then there's what's called a 'strike'
A latch at one point of the rail that closes when you're
not pushing the carcasses fast enough and which
automatically triggers a safety shut down of the entire
slaughter production line

And then
And then the whole upper mezzanine is yelling and
shouting
Their line is blocked so they can't get any more work
done
Except that down below on my own

I'm busting my guts trying to maintain some sort of
rhythm
Except that Tetris is screwing me around and it's never
the pieces you're waiting for that get served up next
It's just shit shit shit
And there's all the yelling from the guys in the slaughter
hall above

But sometimes it's happy days on pre-chilling
It's just after the guys in the slaughter hall have their
break
And there's a half-hour gap in animals to push
Paradise
To be able to hide out and sit down behind a small wall
for a good twenty minutes
Or get ahead so the strike doesn't block and the job
doesn't feel quite so tough

Most often
Which means all the time
I sit down for a minute and then try once more to get
a step ahead of the goddamned relentless advance of
the line

In the pre-chillers
Unlike in my usual coolers
The carcasses are still warm and soft
Rigor mortis does its work
What science defines as 'progressive stiffening of the
musculature caused by irreversible biochemical changes
affecting muscle fibres during the early post-mortem

phase' can be felt in the elasticity and the warmth and
the smell of the animals you're moving
When you try to pack in the animals on a section of rail
to the rear they bounce back due to the cadavers' lack
of rigidity

In the pre-chillers
Right at the start of the 'S' when the animals have just
come down the slaughter-room toboggan
I see a gap as noon approaches and no more cows appear
It's break time for the slaughterers and their crew
We'll soon get half an hour respite
It'll be heaven
I'll be able to skive off for a few minutes sitting down
behind the wall
And get ahead

57.

From time to time they really do give us a laugh at the factory
Every month you're entitled to see the number of workplace injuries and work-related illnesses from the previous month
These figures are recorded and compared with those from the month of the previous year with a green smiley face if the number is down and a red sad face if the number is up
These figures are recorded under a poster where an employee is posing proudly in a beautifully clean work uniform with a slogan doubtless chosen and written out by one of the members of the works council

Thus
We were entitled
Among other *notabilia*

To a social worker declaring 'Try to talk learn to listen remember to reply'
To a nurse declaring 'Treat your injuries – what's best for you is good for everyone'
To an ergonomist declaring 'Rotating jobs is not a lucky dip you're guaranteed a win'

And
Best of all
The one that had us laughing for a good month

A woman on the red offal production line declaring
'Looking for an easy way to pick up
Don't jerk lift slowly'
I remember the morning they put that one up how
We laughed
We laughed
We laughed

'An easy way to pick up'
Yeah right well
It's a good idea really
Let's see you spend a day with us
Dude from the works council
And if you could be so good as to give us your tips on
carrying pushing tugging pulling less
We'd be more up for that than for your dumbass posters

I remember how at one of the factories I used to work in
At the five-minute briefings at the start of the day the
sole purpose of which was to announce the daily
processing targets
One supervisor persisted in asking one of the line
operators to recite the 'four don'ts'

'Don't run in the factory
Don't put your hand in the machinery
Don't climb on the machinery
Do remember to wear your personal protective
equipment'

Not that it takes much to make us laugh
But it put a smile on my face every morning
The fact that there's a 'do' among the 'four don'ts'
But I suppose that's not the point

So this month at the abattoir
Above the month's workplace injuries and work-related illnesses figures
A poster has just appeared that for once isn't the mug of some employee with a catchphrase designed to make us think

Instead it's some cute drawings accompanied by statistics congratulating the group on having reduced the amount of work-related illnesses by forty-seven per cent over seven years due to its health and safety policies

And the reasons for workplace injuries are given alongside little diagrams
1. Handling
Little drawing of a worker lifting a heavy weight marked 'kg'
2. Falls
Little drawing of a worker slipping
3. Cuts
Little drawing of a knife

And for work-related illnesses
1. Back
Little drawing of a back

2. Wrist
Little drawing of a wrist
3. Elbow
Little drawing of an elbow

And while they're congratulating themselves on the reduction in the number of days' sick leave the poster's there announcing in bold no less that this represents more than 21,233 days of work LOST per year for the business
That's me underlining the word 'LOST'

Brendan stopped by this week to say hi at coffee break and tell us how he and his amputated middle finger were going

I'm dreaming about next month's poster
A photo of his hands rather than his smiling dial

'The more fingers I have the better it is'

58.

At the abattoir
On a bad day
You disappear beneath the dead animals being
processed
A mound of bones of offal
Of flesh
Of blood

You don't believe it
You can no longer believe it
A mashed-up mess of a mound

Hallucinations of too many dead animals
Why
For whom

Your back hurts your arms you ache all over but you do
believe it at the end of the day of the month
At the dough earned for our backs our arms our pain
There is that gain
There is the endless night in never-ending corridors

On a good day
There's all that does not weigh so heavily
Our songs
Our words

It's alright when all is said and done
One job is as good as another

And yet
At the abattoir
You believe it
One day
You believe the work will disappear
But when goddamn it
But when

59.

A Monday that starts like shit
A Monday that starts like a week
A shitty Monday that starts the week

In the smokers' shelter the coffee machine has stopped working because of the cold and freezing temperatures
A smoke with no coffee

No time to do the return trip into the bowels of the factory
I head up to the canteen faster than usual to get a shot
A coffee with no smokes

I mutter
It's not a good sign
Not that I'm superstitious but rituals are important
As if
In the Grand Scheme of the factory
Every thing every person every gesture has to be in the same place at the same time
Otherwise everything falls out of synch
It's the theory of the swish of a cow's tail rather than the beating of a butterfly's wing

By way of proof
Heading back down to work
The line doesn't want to get going

It's down for three quarters of an hour with five
hundred and ninety-seven animals to process
Not good at all

So we get going at half past five instead of four forty-five
as planned
You can already smell the overtime that the casuals will
be hit with
The boss arrives at six asks about the delays sees the
extent of the disaster zone in my cool room and pulls a
face as long as the day stretching out before me
He taps me on the shoulder
'Don't worry
I'll come help you push and sort
Each day has enough trouble of its own as they say'

I push my half-carcasses and pinch a nerve or some such
thing
The dead cows are suddenly heavy as a dead horse
There are so many to push and sort

Break
I warn my workmates to get a coffee from the canteen
In the time it takes to cross the huge walkway leading
you outside it's already cold

I sit down on the bench in the smokers' shelter
The twinges of pain are worse now with these cold days
The muscle or the nerve or whatever it is seizes up as it
cools

I wonder just how exactly I'm going to get through
the day
Going back up the stairs of the walkway I'm thinking
I'm never going to make it
But then
When all's said and done you get it done

Back from the break
And it's as bad as ever
It's even worse

Still more sorting more pushing of carcasses and
I'm on my own
The boss isn't there as he promised and I'm never going
to make it
Too many rails and too many animals
And with this pain in my upper-left butt cheek

I don't know how I get to noon
Only one long hour to go
Of pushing mostly
Feels like there's still so much to do

I arrange my carcasses
The muscle-nerve has warmed up with use and is no
longer so painful

Only half an hour more
Just over half an hour
Then just under half an hour
Only another ten minutes

The boss reappears
Sizes up the number of carcasses emptied out that he hasn't sorted
Taps me on the shoulder three times
'Bravo
Good job
Everything that had to be done has been done'

But if only he knew
That I couldn't give a flying fuck about his good job and his empty rails

I've done my work destroyed my back
I bloody killed myself so I would finish in time

There you have it
That's it then

To celebrate I'm going to pig out at the canteen even if my day's finished
Minced steak fried in duck fat with roquefort
There's four of us there from the crew
Nobody speaks except at the end to say
'See you tomorrow'

Outside
Big blue sky
Biting cold

Monday in the sunshine

60.

If I weren't shit-scared about losing this goddamned job
If I had a whistleblower's balls
If youth knew
If age could
If I who am no longer young nor old knew and could
Fuck the havoc I would create in this god-awful abattoir

The day is drawing to an end in the wholesale fridge
The beautiful butchers' beasts
Where I've been assigned for the week
I bring out one last carcass so Guy can break it down
saw it chop it up and prepare it according to the client's
wishes

Suddenly
Commotion of red hard hats on the shop floor
Six at least three of whom I don't recognise

'Guy
Show us how you're doing that'

I try to get closer and yet keep my distance
All very bizarre

The red hard hats are talking among themselves
Talking to Guy
'No
Not like that

Like this
Here have a go and see'

They're holding sheets of paper with anatomical cuts of carcasses split lengthwise and they look stressed

I try to listen but don't hear everything

'Complaint
Seven years' imprisonment and a fine of seven hundred thousand euros
A client who'd sent back carcasses originating from one of the group's factories
The [inaudible] are already onto it
If it gets out if it gets out
Food industry scandal
Bloody hell if it gets out'

I fidget
Damn well give them something to be going on with
Muckraker crew
Oh Upton Sinclair immortal author of the legendary book *The Jungle* from 1905 about Chicago's abattoirs
I'm with you
I'm there

Only an hour to go and I ask Guy some questions
Get a bit of a handle on the thing
Holy cow

I think back to my days of independent journalism to
the good old days when I had a fire in my belly
Article 11
It's not even a topic anymore
It's a bomb

Back home
A few searches on the internet
Everything bears out
I take notes
I revel
And tomorrow
I'll investigate

Yes but the next day
I'm missing two essential pieces of information
The name of the factory in the group and that of the
supermarket client

I'm struggling to imagine myself
Going to see one of the big bosses small time casual that
I am
'So yeah it's a bit of a worry this business
But tell me which factory in the group is it and which
client'

Might as well be grilled good and proper like a side of
beef at a summer barbeque if the info gets out

So what then
Wait

Not wanting to lose your job going on a fishing
expedition that's doomed from the get-go
And yet I have all the logical pieces of a great outrage

'An argument is an idea plus an example'
So my good Jesuit teachers used to say to me
Over and over

Except that now
I've got the idea
But no solid example of the stuff-up

So I shut my trap and become complicit in a food
scandal
Lack of balls
Spinelessly I wait for fear of losing my job

If only I had those two extra pieces of information
If only
If only I saw

With saws
You cut wood
And Guy cuts carcasses

The bosses are scared witless and I am too
Everything's fine
The food processing industry continues to forge ahead

We're all stuck in our own semi-circle of shit and
shackles
To each his own shit

61.

On my way to work I wonder who the patron saints
of workers and butchers are

Racking my brains
Having been quite fond of a few saints over the years

Saint Francis of Assisi
The wealthy guy who throws it all in and goes off to talk
to the birds
Saint Roch and his dog as invoked by my grandmother
when I would cling to her like glue
Which is to say all the time
Saint Anthony of Padua for the retrieval of lost objects
Saint Rita inevitably

Having no idea I park the notion until knock-off time
when I can get back to my computer

It's a mindless day as only the factory knows how to
turn on

No *deus ex* to intervene in the inexorable progress
of the production line and the continuing waves of
carcasses
No break downs

And so many things to do once I get home

Re-register myself at the unemployment agency seeing as I'd dropped off the bastards' list this month for whatever reason
See I'm a dole bludger even though I'm a regular casual at the factory so don't count on me to bring down the jobless figures

Call the temp agency to get an advance until the end of the week

Do some banking stuff

Once I'm home from work I switch on the computer and look up the patron saints who've been bugging me all day
'Patron saint of butchers: Saint Bartholomew'
Worse than a slaughter
A massacre
'Symbol: his own flayed skin.
Bartholomew wears the hide of his own flayed skin because he was also skinned alive. He is sometimes depicted holding the large knife used to inflict this torture.'

And next

'Patron saint of workers: Saint Joseph (...) Some Catholics entrust to his prayers their important worldly issues such as looking for a job, etc.'

Ora et labora

62.

It’s audit day
The full catastrophe

I don’t know what big-shot client or official regulator or
Joe Bloggs is coming to visit the factory today but
everything has to be spick and span from seven in the
morning
So it sounds like we’ll be working in a Potemkin factory

We’ll have had a solid two hours to stash away the
purulent carcasses they don’t want displayed
Stash into pockets or boots the big protective gloves
that we nonetheless use every day
Scrub the floor the walls the stainless steel even the
plastic cords we use to work the switch plates on our
rails
Clean up the mess so typical of the factory so it looks
like it’s some fairytale of hygiene and safety

And in the meantime
We’re meant to handle the processing
‘Because it’s a big day’
The bosses say

And most importantly manage the audit
‘Because it’s a big audit’
Say the bosses freaking out

Bosses
It's the same every audit
You never see so much of them
And especially never see so much of them actually working
As they do on those days

It's a ballet of red hard hats
They get involved in the work
Shift carcasses
Clean up as well instead of delegating as usual to the casual cleaning crew

You have to see it from their point of view
The bosses' that is
Fuck up the audit
The production line closes
And they can start looking for another job

The red hard hats carry on frantically with their phone calls and their fussing
'The auditors are coming
The auditors are coming'
Accompanied by four senior red hard hats
Two female and one male auditor listen dutifully to the bosses' explanations
Ask a few vague questions of some hand-picked line operators
Only five more minutes to go
Then they're off

When the auditors have gone back up the stairs taking
them to the factory's 'guest restaurant'
We'll bring our shitty carcasses back out
Like any other day we won't give a damn about the
so-called hygiene and health and safety requirements
that just ten minutes ago were so important
We'll put our gloves back on
After the auditors have taken their time walking around
the shop floor we'll start back on the rails we had kept
empty
Start back on the treadmill

63.

I've got Sunday-itis
Those goddamned Sunday evening blues before
heading back to the coalface

Tomorrow
At six in the morning
I'll have finished drinking my coffee and eating my
two slices of toast with salted butter
And have walked the mutt
I'll be about to get in the car for the twenty-minute
drive
Fifteen minutes in the smokers' shelter with another
coffee and my two smokes before clocking on
Before descending into the hellhole that is the
abattoir

Tomorrow
At six in the morning
In all likelihood
They'll be sending in the troops at the deferred
development
zone at Notre-Dame-des-Landes
I won't be there

Since Friday
I've been reading all the papers looking at all the
websites

It's happening
All hell's going to break loose

I could have been there
I hesitated on Friday and Saturday
Do I ditch everything for a week and join my mates
Give Kéru from Groix a call
The guy who set up squats on his pebble of an island
and has been living there for years

Thought about my old workmate Greg from my
teaching days who'd lived there after years in Nicaragua
seeing out the end of the Sandinistas then living in the
squats of Turin and with whom I'd experienced the epic
savage demos of 2006 against the 'first employment
contract' laws in Nanterre and Paris
How we smashed things up
And how we laughed
He would tell me too about his epic memories of the
protests against the Devaquet higher education laws
That carnage at Les Invalides in 1986 when they held
the bridge as Malik Oussekine lay dying not far away
under Pasqua's bludgeons

Greg threw himself under an RER train at Saint-Michel
five years later I think
I remember his cremation at Père Lachaise where we
would walk before he died stopping for a beer at the
Communards' Wall every time
At his funeral

A dozen of his mates from Notre-Dame-des-Landes had come
And climbing the steps of the crematorium
I heard the most stirring rendition of *The Bloody Week*
I've ever heard and sang along with dishevelled young twenty-year-olds both male and female to whom he had taught the song

We climbed up onto the wall
Brought out our beers
Singing it over and over
'Yes but
You can feel the change a-coming
The bad old days will end
And be wary of revenge
When the poor will rise again'

Yes but
Tomorrow I have to work

And look at me
The little casual
The part-time anarchist
I'm choosing work
I don't have enough dosh to be able to take off for a week to somewhere not even two hours away by car

And yet
Would I not have been more useful there
Writing one hell of a story
A killer text I'm sure

About eviction
The rage the revolt the doubts of some and the certainty of others

Doing what I'm supposed to be doing
Not necessarily manning a barricade
But writing something other than the factory

I belong to the reserve army which the great Karl talks about in his *Wage Labour and Capital* as early as 1847
'Big industry constantly requires a reserve army of unemployed workers for times of overproduction. The main purpose of the bourgeois in relation to the worker is, of course, to have the commodity labour as cheaply as possible, which is only possible when the supply of this commodity is as large as possible in relation to the demand for it, i.e. when the overpopulation is the greatest.'
That army of unemployed workers happy to be casuals.

If tomorrow
At Lorient
There were a massive demo of rioting protesters
In support of the deferred development zone of the railway workers the students the nurses and all the rest who struggle against this world and where it's all heading
If I had the time and energy to go and protest
To smash in some windows again of banks of real estate agencies of temp agencies
Of course

Standing in front of my own agency
I'd be there with the guys in their balaclavas saying
'Not them
They're decent
They feed me work'

The wonder of voluntary servitude
The misery of Sundays
The bad old days will come to an end

64.

'You don't learn a thing
At poetry school
You fight'

Léo Ferré
Preface

Mum

Here
By way of preface
It could be said that at factory school
You don't learn anything either
You fight

And that at cancer school
It's just the same
You fight
We're going to fight

Yesterday the official news was handed down
It fell
As you risk falling and injuring yourself if you don't watch out
For anaemia
For the white blood cells
For the fractures of your vertebrae that have given you so much grief for months

And to all this
We can finally put a name
Myeloma
Cancer of the bone marrow

Of course we had a small suspicion
When we came to Reims for those four days
Before your appointment with the haematologist
But of course we did not suspect
Your pain
And your strength

You took a good half-day to ask me for my arm
Just
To help you
Stand up

We did not suspect
During our usual Sunday phone calls
When you would say
'I'm in a bit of pain'
That things had come to this

At cancer school
You're not prepared

The memory of your mother
Of my grandmother
That story you told me which I hadn't known
That when the oncologist had told her the news
She in her eternal wisdom said

‘Well when all is said and done I’ll die from this
Or something else’

And your strength yesterday on the telephone
And your cheerfulness
And your jokes
‘There are thousands and thousands and thousands
What am I saying
Millions
Of people living with cancer’

I think back on the chat we had that weekend about
my job
Of course it’s hardly perfect
It can often be a bit hellish
It’s tough and painful and annoying
But that’s how it is

If I start telling myself that it’s the worst thing that
could happen to me this factory job
Sure I’d blow my top and go completely crazy
But no
It is how it is and I’m not complaining
Except for sometimes about my back and how tired I am
And I laugh at the great absurdity of this working life
I’m learning nothing
But I’m fighting
Fighting the pace the time the pain
Fighting myself
In fact I am learning

But of your cancer we will learn nothing
We will battle
The pain
The anxiety of the waiting for results
The chemo and the sterile hospital room where you'll stay perhaps a while
We will learn

We will learn that we have in fact been strong
We have not been complacent
That we are here
For good
No matter what happens
That love
Preserves everything
No matter what happens

One sole regret
That I'm no longer working in the fish crustacean and shellfish factory
Like I was over a year ago
I would dearly have loved to stuff myself with a shitload of crab on the sly

Strength
Courage
Endurance

Your son who loves you

65.

And all those lines I didn't write
Though written in my mind a thousand times on my production lines
Phrases both beautiful and profound
Linking one to the next
Relentlessly

Where Alexandrines to match those of Victor Hugo rang out
Addressed as much to the machines as to humanity

Dreamlike sonnets

I must have even managed to rhyme
Slaughter to mortar
Crustacean to flirtation
Processing plant to Kant

But
No sooner am I home
Drunk from exhaustion and the few drinks I've downed after work
All is forgotten

Facing down the expanse of the daily grind
There's nothing but the euphoria of rest
And chores to do

One passage of text
Means two hours
Two hours stolen from resting from eating from
showering from walking the dog

I have written so much in my head then forgotten
Perfect phrases that described
That circumscribed my work

I have written and stolen two hours from daily life
From this shared life with my wife
Hours at the factory
Words and hours
Like so many stolen kisses
Like so much happiness

And all those words I didn't write

66.

My wife my love

There is that poem by Apollinaire from the trenches
that haunts me with its beauty and its truth

'There is a ship that has borne my beloved away
There is a sky in which six sausage blimps hang maggot-
like yet might they give birth to stars as night approaches
There is an enemy submarine with my love in its sights'

There is that song by Vanessa Paradis
The second one played at our wedding to open the
dancing that I've been humming all day

'There is lalala
If we took our time
If we took our time
There is literature there
The lack of desire
The inertia the movement'

There is your birthday on this Maundy Thursday

There is the abattoir where I will return tomorrow
morning and the boarding house at the girls' school
where you'll work until eleven o'clock at night by which
time I'll be long fast asleep

There is this gift I want to write for you

There are the cows in the lairage waiting to be killed
tomorrow at the crack of dawn

There are the kids in Venezuela or Madagascar who are
preparing crowns of frozen prawns

There is Peter who this very night before the crowing of
the rooster will have three times denied knowing Jesus
but still he swears to his master
No

There are some flowers and a parcel from your mum-in-
law waiting for when you get home

There is the cleaning crew with their chemicals and gas
masks who will as they do every Thursday come
through the wholesale fridge where I worked today and
which we emptied out specially

There is always one poet from the lists I try to
remember to help me pass the time from the
Renaissance group of poets known as *Les Pléiades*
whose name I forget

Pierre de Ronsard Joachim Du Bellay Étienne
Jodelle Antoine de Baïf Rémy Belleau Pontus de Tyard

There is the fact that today I felt strong and was able to lift from their hooks without too much difficulty the fifty-odd lambs that had been ordered for Easter

There is the crumbed-fish factory that runs on an endless schedule of three eight-hour shifts and the men and women inside who are already waiting for changeover which will happen at exactly eight o'clock in the evening

There is our love

There is my forebear Pontus de Tyard and two of his lines of verse that fit so well with these notes from a factory
'That incessantly and in all humility
My words shall honour and my spirit contemplate'

There is our dog Pok Pok who's napping peacefully on the sofa after our walk

There is the feeling of being too lazy to cook and the no place to park outside the bakery to buy some sliced bread so it'll be Livarot cheese and ham with no bread

There is the labourer at the lairage who cleans up the dung from the cows waiting to be killed the next day

There is the sirloin with fries and béarnaise sauce I ate in the canteen at noon with a mineral water for four euros eighty-five deducted from my pay

There are people who right now are eating crumbed fish
and prawns or steaks without the slightest idea

There is the fact that even knowing what I know I eat
steak

There is the fact that 'it is all quite macabre and in the
face of such a ghastly evocation I don't know what else
to say'

There is the fact we won't see each other to celebrate
on your birthday but instead tomorrow for a three-and-
a-half-day weekend

There is the final chorus of Bach's *St Matthew Passion*
that I'm listening to as I write these words to you

There is the stale bread I've just found to make myself a
little sandwich

There are my dirty nails the stinking body I can no
longer even smell and the shower I've not yet had

'There is the love that carries me gently away'

There are men in the world who have never been in a
factory nor ever been to war

'There are mysteries over there and silence'

There is the fact that tomorrow I'll pay dearly for these
words I've stayed up so late to write

There are factories I know nothing about producing
green beans weapons potato chips cars nitrate drinking
chocolate fabric papier mâché or Armenian paper and
all the people inside them

There is as much happiness as there is back pain and
exhaustion

There is the fact that I must put this final full stop
To the line
And return

There is this birthday present which I want to finish
writing for you

There is the fact that there will never be
Even if I find a real job
Insofar as the factory is a fake one
Which I doubt

There is the fact that there will never be
Any
Final full stop
On the line

THANK YOU

To Alice and Jérôme for the trust and the joy

To Manon Anne Marc Mohamad and Adam
for lending me their car or car-pooling with me
so I could get to work every morning

To the good fairies at the temp agency
Audrey Charlotte Mathilde and Manon
Christelle and Vanessa

To Jean-Michel and Jean-Marc
Without whose never-repeated olfactory refusals none of this would have been possible

To Coralie Isabelle and Jane
For the words and readings

To Xavier
For *The Hope and Fear*

To the loyal and devoted group from the great virtual social network
Pénélope Heptanes Marie-Aude and Ingrid

To the loyal and devoted gang from the real world
Christophe Jean-Guillaume Sonya Marie-Anne Lolo

Jennifer and Denis Emma and Dadu Myriam and Guillaume Hermann Sandrine Jean-Charles Aude-Marie Élodie Manu Christiane and Roger Céline and Pierre Aouatif Dora and Alexis Evina and Laurent Nolwenn Claudine and Éric

To Gaëlle
For the care

To Gustavo #10
For the Cyclone and the Merlus

To the women and men on prawns at the fish market on unloading processing preparation cleaning on direct-to-public wholesaling quartering deboning and loading Brigitte Frank Fabien Richard Mourad Fanfan Manu Julien Fabrice Bénédicte Riad Denis Guy Morgan the two Sébs Fabrice Antoine Jean-Pierre Brendan Nico Patrice Michel Bernard Stéphane Franck Christian Philippe Jacques Jean-Luc Serge Joël Pascal Cyril Chérif Diaby Abdy and the women and men whom I'm forgetting and some of the bosses too Christophe Enguerrand Narong Éric Yohan Jean-Paul and Philou

To Catherine
For the super cool summer job with the Down syndrome vacationers

To the workers in this book who bring these pages alive

To Luther Blisset
For the inspiration

To Blaise Thierry Guillaume Louis René and Séb for Bertolt and for life

To my family
In Reims and Houat and everywhere else

ENDNOTES

Pages 19–20 'FLN/OAS' *Front de Libération Nationale* or *National Liberation Front*: a political movement established in Algeria in 1954 to oppose the continuing French colonial presence in that country.

Organisation de l'armée secrète or *Secret Army Organisation*: a right-wing paramilitary organisation founded in 1961 that engaged in terrorist methods to oppose Algerian independence.

Page 43 'Marie-Louise conscripts': a term coined to describe young recruits to the Napoleonic wars who were used to defend against the allied invasion of France in 1813–14. They were so named after Empress Marie-Louise, who signed the relevant conscription decree. The term was again used in World War I to describe young conscripts into the armed forces.

Page 50 'Agnès Saal': a senior civil servant who was made to step down from her position as head of the National Audiovisual Institute amid allegations of excessive expenditure on taxi services, a portion of which she admitted had been incurred by her son.

Page 64 'the familistery of Guise': A *familistery* or *familistere* is a community of workers and their families. The author is referring to one such community, established by Jean-Baptiste Godin in the 19th century at his factory in Guise, which included services such as a crèche, hospital and shops as well as housing.

Page 118 'Cendrars': Blaise Cendrars (1887–1961), Swiss-born author, poet and art critic who lost his right arm in World War I while serving in the Foreign Legion.

Page 136 'The Song of Craonne' or *Chanson de Craonne*: One of the most famous anti-war songs in France. It is generally understood to have been sung by the soldiers who mutinied after the disastrous Nivelle Offensive in 1917.

Page 149 'Fernand Braudel': a prominent historian and academic (1902–1985) known, among other things, for developing a historical theory that considered vast geographical areas through the lens of a three-tiered time-scale, namely the *longue durée* or *long term,* the *middle term* and the *short term*. The author is referring to Braudel's *La Méditerranée et le monde méditerranéen à l'époque de Philippe II* (*The Mediterranean and the Mediterranean World in the Age of Philip II*).

Page 157 'CGT': the acronym for the *Confédération Générale du Travail,* otherwise known as the French General Confederation of Labour union.

Page 158 'Manu': French president Emmanuel Macron is sometimes referred to as Manu.

Page 174 'The bawdy songs': This paragraph is a compilation of lines from some traditional French drinking songs, namely *La grosse bite à Dudule* (*Dudule's Big Dick*),

Les filles de Camaret (*The Girls from Camaret*), *Fanchon* and *Le petit vin blanc* (*A Little White Wine*).

Page 190 'L.214': Ethics and Animals L.214 is a non-profit organisation that raises awareness of conditions surrounding the exploitation of animals for human consumption. Its name is a reference to Article L.214 of the French *Rural Code*, which provides: 'Every animal is a sentient being and shall accordingly be kept by its owner in conditions compatible with the biological imperatives of its species.'

Page 218 'Article 11': A reference to Article 11 of the French 1789 *Declaration of the Rights of Man and of the Citizen*, which provides: 'The free communication of ideas and opinions is one of the most precious of the rights of man. Every citizen may, accordingly, speak, write and print with freedom, but shall be responsible for such abuses of this freedom as shall be defined by law.'

Page 226 'Notre-Dame-des-Landes': One of the most well-known political squats in France, where activists have taken up residence on the site of a deferred development zone for a proposed airport since 2008.

Page 227 'Malik Oussekine' and Charles 'Pasqua': Malik Oussekine died after being beaten by French police during demonstrations against higher education reforms (known as the Devaquet reforms, after the then deputy minister for education, Alain Devaquet). Charles Pasqua was minister of the interior at the time and responsible for police.

Praise for *On the Line*

'Poetic and political, lyrical and realistic, Joseph Ponthus' spirited elegy is at once surprising, captivating and affecting.' *Télérama*

'It is not every day that one witnesses the birth of a writer.' *France 5 La Grande Librairie*

'A work that is powerful, clever, benevolent, optimistic even. Essential reading.' *Causette*

'A major literary work, the first revelation for 2019.' *RTL Laissez-vous tenter*

'A cantata of a book that exudes vitality.' *La Croix*

'The sensation of the literary season.' *Grazia*

'A hard-hitting work, flabbergasting, unprecedented, written entirely in unbridled verse, a sort of Victor Hugo–like fable of the ages depicting the present day.' *Siné Mensuel*

'Joseph Ponthus has positioned himself as one of the great authors of our times with his arrival on the literary scene.' *L'Alsace*

'Truly astonishing, succinct, powerful, enthralling.' *CNews Matin*

'*On the Line* is not just an extraordinary debut novel, it is also a hard-hitting work that is, dare I say it, essential.' *L'Express*

'A powerful work.' *Le Point*

'A literary tour de force.' *Bretons*

After studying literature and social work, **Joseph Ponthus** worked for over ten years as a social worker and special needs teacher in the suburbs of Paris. In 2012 he co-authored *Nous … La Cité* (*The Suburbs Are Ours*). He lives and works in Brittany, France.

Stephanie Smee left a career in law to work as a literary translator. Recent translations include Hannelore Cayre's *The Inheritors* and *The Godmother* (winner of the CWA Crime Fiction in Translation Dagger award), and Françoise Frenkel's rediscovered World War II memoir, *No Place to Lay One's Head*, which was awarded the JQ–Wingate Prize. Her translation of Pascal Janovjak's *The Rome Zoo* is forthcoming.